A Soviet Postmortem

A Soviet Postmortem

Philosophical Roots of the "Grand Failure"

Sigmund Krancberg

with a foreword by
Wilson Carey McWilliams

Rowman & Littlefield Publishers, Inc.

ROWMAN & LITTLEFIELD PUBLISHERS, INC.

Published in the United States of America
by Rowman & Littlefield Publishers, Inc.
4720 Boston Way, Lanham, Maryland 20706

3 Henrietta Street
London, WC2E 8LU, England

Copyright © 1994 by Rowman & Littlefield Publishers, Inc.

All rights reserved. No part of this publication may be reproduced, stored in a retrieval system, or transmitted in any form or by any means, electronic, mechanical, photocopying, recording, or otherwise, without the prior permission of the publisher.

British Cataloging in Publication Information Available

Library of Congress Cataloging-in-Publication Data

Krancberg, Sigmund.
A Soviet postmortem : philosophical roots of the "Grand Failure" / by Sigmund Krancberg ; with a foreword by Wilson Carey McWilliams.
p. cm.
Includes bibliographical references and index.
1. Communism—Soviet Union. 2. Soviet Union—Politics and government. 3. Soviet Union—Intellectual life. I. Title.
HX311.5.K73   1994   335.43'0947—dc20   94-15332   CIP

ISBN 0-8476-7927-6 (cloth : alk. paper)
ISBN 0-8476-7928-4 (pbk. : alk. paper)

Part of Chapter 1 appeared in a different form in "1984: The Totalitarian Model Revisited," *Studies in Soviet Thought* 29 (1985): 71–77; part of Chapter 3 appeared as "Karl Marx and Democracy," in *Studies in Soviet Thought* 24 (1985): 23-35; and an earlier version of Chapter 4 appeared as "Controlling Individual Development and Behavior," *Studies in Soviet Thought* 27 (1984): 319–34. All © D. Reidel Publishing Company, and reprinted here with the permission of Kluwer Academic Publishers.
    An earlier version of Chapter 2 appeared as "The Unity of Theory and Practice in Historical Perspective," in *Studies in Soviet Thought* 41 (1991): 173–205, © Sigmund Krancberg.
    An earlier version of Chapter 5 appeared as "Soviet Philosophy," in *Survey* 28, no. 3 (Autumn 1984): 157–72, © *Survey* (no longer published).

Printed in the United States of America

∞™ The paper used in this publication meets the minimum requirements of American National Standard for Information Sciences—Permanence of Paper for Printed Library Materials, ANSI Z39.48–1984.

Dedication

To my beloved wife, Livia,
my first, last, and perpetual inspiration,
and
our beloved daughters, Shelly and Beth,
and
our precious granddaughter, Amy Rose.

Contents

Acknowledgments		ix
Foreword	*by Wilson Carey McWilliams*	xi

Part One   **A Reappraisal of the Totalitarian Model: The Vertical Concepts**

1	Western Sovietology in Crisis	3

Part Two   **A Reappraisal of the Totalitarian Model: The Horizontal Concepts**

2	The Unity of Theory and Practice in Historical Perspective	33
3	The Corruption of Democratic Principles	65
4	Controlling Individual Development and Behavior	93
5	Soviet Philosophy	109
6	The Profile of an Empire: The World Socialist System	129
7	Conclusion: The Disintegration of the Soviet Union and the Journey into the Unknown	139
Postscript		161
Index		163
About the Author		169

Acknowledgments

I want to acknowledge a large intellectual debt to Wilson Carey McWilliams, who made many helpful and illuminating comments and who has written the foreword to this book. I am equally indebted to Charles H. Fairbanks, Jr., for his critical and valuable suggestions on the manuscript.

I want to express my gratitude to the Lynde and Harry G. Bradley Foundation for supporting my research, with particular thanks to Dr. Hillel Fradkin.

Also special thanks to our daughter Beth Krancberg and Nancy Middleton for their priceless gift of a computer, without which I would still be working on my fifty-year-old manual Remington typewriter. Also very important were Jennifer Norris's ceaseless lessons and patience in teaching me how to use the computer.

My thanks also go to my friend and editor Sheila Clark, as well as to my friend David Schwartz for his comments. I would also like to thank Joanna Lee Mullins for her copyediting of the manuscript.

But most of all, I am deeply grateful to my wife, Livia, whose unfailing support, encouragement, patience, and understanding make my life more meaningful with each year that passes.

Sigmund Krancberg

Foreword

Sigmund Krancberg has written an admirable book, especially valuable for contemporary students. The Soviet experiment is now a closed chapter in human history, but the *lesson* of Soviet failure speaks to the broader and perennial temptations of human pride. The Soviet Union began with heroic aspiration pursued with ruthless dedication, a titanic and epochal attempt to remake humanity through state power and terror. By the end, however, revolutionary vision had been reduced to bureaucratic routine, a "road to nowhere" in which power seemed its own end. Krancberg is an ideal analyst of the Soviet tragedy and farce; his fine scholarship is deepened by his personal encounters with political evil. A champion of decency and common sense, scornful of pretense and self-deception, Krancberg argues forcefully and with warmth, and all these qualities are needed to pierce the disguises of Soviet political history.

There has never been a shortage of explanations for the shortcomings of the USSR. The simplest holds, for example, that socialism was betrayed by Stalin, who undermined Lenin's more positive legacy.[1] A more searching argument contends that the Soviet Union was doomed from the outset because still-backward Russia was not ready for socialism on Marx's terms. Marxian socialism presumes economic development, but the Soviet government was forced to attempt to produce development by *force majeure*, repression overruling frustration.[2] Although there is an element of truth in such arguments, Krancberg recognizes their fundamental inadequacy: at bottom, the "grand failure"[3] of the Soviet experiment is rooted in its theory, in the flaws of Marxism itself, and specifically, in Marx's view of the relation between thought and practice.

Ancient political philosophy regarded theory and practice as related but distinct, uneasy yokefellows often inclined to pull in different directions. By reflection and dialogue, human beings can discern the best life and the best politics possible within the limits of nature, but the ability to bring the best *polis* into existence in speech does not imply the possibility to realize it in action. In Plato's *Republic*, Socrates suggests that the best city could come into being only if a philosopher were allowed to build a public from the ground up, beginning with children no older than ten. And even the possibilities of speech are limited by the wisdom and virtue of the speakers.

Political practice, in the ancient view, is always constrained and limited by circumstances that human beings do not control. Political life is premised on givens; laws and policies must be adapted to specific peoples, places, and times. In American politics, for example, laws and policies that *best* protect the environment are not practicable: we can hope only for policies that do as well as they can, given our dependence on the automobile and on industrial civilization generally. Similarly, race relations would be easier if slavery and oppression had not been the themes of our past, but the past cannot be rewritten; we can only try to compensate for what cannot be undone.

Theory, the quest to discover what is best, is a kind of voyage beyond the boundaries of convention and practicality. Yet, the ancients argued, practical politics needs the standard of theory in the same way that pilots need stars to steer by. To know what is best within a set of circumstances, we need to have some idea of what simply is best. Theory is the guide and critic of practice, forever necessary in reminding citizens and leaders of the ways in which their politics falls short of the ideal.

By contrast, modern political philosophy, following the path indicated by Niccolo Machiavelli and Francis Bacon, argued that political circumstance can, in large measure, be anticipated and controlled. Human beings can master nature and chance by understanding and using nature's own forces, a new science that conceives a politics founded on the aspects of human nature that are reliable and universal, though low—the passions and, especially, the desire for safety and for gain.[4] Modern political philosophy, in other words, blurred the line between theory and practice: in its new terms, the truth that matters is not what is best but what works—*la verita effettuale*, Machiavelli said—so that theory came to be regarded as an understanding of practice, the ways in which nature can be channeled toward human ends, a road map to the liberation of humanity from nature's restraint.[5]

However, for the founders of modern political philosophy, *human* nature remained a given, just as the human subject was distinct from the natural object it sought to master. The American founders, the most successful students of eighteenth-century political science, proclaimed that human rights are "inalienable," part of an equality and an endowment that human beings did not choose and cannot undo.

As Krancberg observes, it became increasingly fashionable in the nineteenth century (and since) to argue that any idea of a fixed human nature is repugnant to freedom, which requires that human beings be free to make themselves. Beginning with Hegel's contention that consciousness is developed in history, Marx went on to argue that consciousness is itself not above but in history, a product that human beings make. Of course, Marx recognized and taught that even if human beings make history, they do not "make it as they please"; humanity is constrained by the laws of historical conflict and change.[6] But as Krancberg shows, Marx's view presumes that human productive activity in history progressively frees humanity from even *historical* necessity, although this liberation is concealed or distorted by the societies with which it is associated. In its conflict with capitalism, the proletariat pursues what it takes to be its interest; Marxist theory discerns—or so Marx imagined—that the logic of proletarian politics points to the ultimate liberation of humankind.

Krancberg indicates the paradox of this thesis. The great teachers of the Enlightenment, like the founders of modern political philosophy, hoped for a science by which the human psyche could direct history, where inward freedom translated into outward practice, just as Hobbes's social contract aspired to establish *in foro externo* the laws of nature already discerned *in foro interno*.[7] In Marx's doctrine, by contrast, human activity shapes the soul, so that what had been regarded as a directive force becomes an object, and freedom itself is reduced to an artifact. Marx, in other words, offered a theoretical argument that asserts the supremacy of practice over the theoretical faculty. In Marxism, theory contrives to subordinate itself, humbling consciousness on the anvil of history. And without a sense that nature—or at least, human nature—sets limits to what is possible and proper, Marxism pointed toward a moral nihilism in practice; as Krancberg notes, Marx accepted war and terror in the interest of transforming workers themselves.

In Soviet life, Krancberg demonstrates, this subjugation of theory to practice was carried to its extreme. Theory became ideology in the pure sense, a justification for the regime.[8] In the Soviet context, this implied that theory/ideology should justify revolutionary action: *Praxis* did not refer to the realities of Russian or Soviet life and culture, but to an imposition on that life and culture, the means chosen by the Communist Party to defend its position and to further its professional goal of transformation. Soviet doctrine, in other words, lacked *both* a critical perspective on the regime *and* an appreciation of the real limits of practice, the inertias of Russian and Soviet life.

Few writers even approximate Krancberg's skill in helping us understand the operations—so pervasive yet so superficial—of party and ideology in Soviet political life. As Krancberg demonstrates, Western social science, a few praiseworthy exceptions aside, failed to understand the nature and fragility of Soviet politics. In the first place, social scientists, over-inclined by their training to discount ideas and to focus on behavior, sought to explain the USSR by reference to the sort of objective data and measures conventionally relied on in the West. They neglected, Krancberg indicates, the fact that in a regime such as the Soviet Union, all such data are appearances, conditioned by doctrine and the character of the regime—useful clues, but in need of deep interpretation. In the Soviet party state, virtually all information had a political purpose, and the Soviet public learned to hear *through* the data, just as it learned to respond in terms shaped by official doctrine. As that suggests, Western social science underrated the pervasive quality of ideology under Soviet rule. It saw the driving, hierarchical force of *vertical* totalitarianism, especially under Stalin, and it recognized that, post-Stalin, *vertical* totalitarianism softened into administration. But—and this is Krancberg's very special insight—it tended to overlook *horizontal* totalitarianism, the persistence of ideology in the thought and day-to-day premises that shaped the conduct of Soviet officialdom.

Krancberg's analysis helps explain the Communist Party's inertial resistance to *perestroika*. It also indicates that Gorbachev, a devoted socialist, also clung to the party because he recognized how fragile the Soviet Union would be without the party's constraint. Surely, what is most striking about the Communist Party's seventy years of rule is how little it achieved in overcoming the older solidarities of ethnicity. In the end, Soviet teaching failed in practice and as theory.

The essence of all totalitarianism lies in the belief that the truth is something we create or construct, not something we discern or discover, because that premise implies that humanity can be remade if power can be united with will. This set of convictions has outlived the fall of the Soviet Union as it outlasted Nazism. The West is politically triumphant, but its intellectual life is pervaded by doctrines which assert that truth is only an artifact of culture or language, a tool of power. Turned against established authority, such notions can seem liberative, especially to the young, and part of the value of Krancberg's book lies in revealing their darker logic. Krancberg knows that the real limit on authority also limits rebellion against authority;

we are all held to the measure of truth and the mirror of nature. The Soviet failure can serve to remind us that all regimes and peoples need theory in its proper office, as the critic and conscience of practice.

Wilson Carey McWilliams
Rutgers University

Notes

1. Leon Trotsky, *The Revolution Betrayed* (New York: Doubleday, Doran & Co., 1937).

2. John Plamenatz, *German Marxism and Russian Communism* (London: Longmans, Green & Co., 1954).

3. The phrase "grand failure" is taken from Zbigniew Brzezinski, *The Grand Failure* (New York: Charles Scribner & Sons, 1989).

4. Norman Jacobson, "Political Science Review and Political Education," *American Political Science Review*, LVII (1963): 561–69; Leo Strauss, *Natural Right and History* (Chicago: University of Chicago Press, 1953), 165–251.

5. Machiavelli, *The Prince*, chap. XV; Immanuel Kant, *On the Old Saw: That May Be Right in Theory, but It Won't Work in Practice*, E.B. Ashton, trans. (Philadelphia: University of Pennsylvania Press, 1974).

6. *The Eighteenth Brumaire of Louis Bonaparte*, in Karl Marx and Friedrich Engels, *Selected Works* (Moscow, 1935), vol. I, 247.

7. Thomas Hobbes, *Leviathan*, chap. XV.

8. Karl Mannheim, *Ideology and Utopia* (New York: Harcourt Brace & Co., 1956), esp. pp. 239–47, 250.

Part One

A Reappraisal of the Totalitarian Model: The Vertical Concepts

1

Western Sovietology in Crisis

> The health of Soviet society is very sound, and the ailments common to capitalism are unknown to it. In the USSR there are no social grounds for individualism, money grubbing, parasitism, and other manifestations of bourgeois morality.
>
> *Social Science* (Moscow: 1977), Progress Publishers[1]

> How fascinating to live long enough to meet one's own world as history, and find it barely recognizable.
>
> Malcolm Muggeridge

In the winter of 1990, *Daedalus*, the prestigious journal of the American Academy of Arts and Sciences, published a comprehensive and well-argued essay "To the Stalin Mausoleum"[2] signed by Z. Because of the momentous events unfolding in the Soviet Union, this essay represents a rare piece of writing and its first merit is that the author—later identified as Martin Malia, professor of Russian history at the University of California at Berkeley—succeeds in rectifying past and current misconceptions of Western Sovietologists as seen through the critical spectacles of an expert historian. Its second merit is that Z. chooses to focus on the idea of *perestroika* evaluated from a political perspective, contemplated not just as a "reform in the ordinary sense of organization" but as a substantial and analytic inquiry into the "systemic crisis of Sovietism *per se*."[3]

It is more than coincidental that, reflecting on seventy years of political hysteria, constant fear, mindlessness, hypocrisy, loss of faith, and emptiness,[4] Russian publicists are likewise searching for answers to the pressing question "Why did we build in such a way that it is now necessary to rebuild?" And pondering the tragic political experience of Soviet Communism, the publicists call for a moral cleansing, a "moral self-purification of each person and the society as a whole,"[5] in the fervent hope that the demise of Marxist-Leninist ideology will herald a genuine renewal of all aspects of life. In this widespread and painful process of soulsearching, concomitant to a relentless questioning of historical facts, free of distortion and forgery, Lenin and his policies are singled out as largely responsible for creating the suffocating and oppressive atmosphere of a police state in post-revolutionary Russia. This strong, pioneering spirit of nonconformism surfaced openly in 1988 in an article written by Vasily Selyunin,[6] in which he defiantly linked Lenin to the inauguration of indiscriminate terror, forced labor camps, and collectivization. In an interview with David Remnick, the Moscow correspondent to the *Washington Post* from January 1988 to September 1991, Selyunin declared that "the idea was to write a piece so that people would begin to realize that the system itself was *stillborn,* that we could not blame everything on the devil image of Stalin" (emphasis added).[7]

A year later, the prominent Russian philosopher Igor Klyamkin, stated:

> Leninist policies pretended to serve the "truth" while consigning to the dustbin of history the pack of "bourgeois lies." In actuality, Leninist policies turned into a cynical disarticulation of elementary images of good and evil in a violent process never before experienced in the civilized world.[8]

Disregarding throughout the years the many symptoms of endemic corruption, decay, and mismanagement on all levels of the Soviet government, Western Sovietologists portrayed the Soviet Union as a country undergoing a process of industrial development and transformation by way of modernization and urbanization in a milieu of achievements in modern science and technology. As David Remnick observed, "no other modern society has ever done more to suppress, to manipulate, its own history, and sustained the effort for so long."[9] As a result of this historically unprecedented deception, Sovietologists understated the fact that the rapid and huge industrialization process was a distinctly one-sided enterprise, favoring heavy industry without any consideration whatsoever for the ecology of the environment; that it was a process which, in reality, jeopardized the country's agriculture, the food industry, and consumer goods production, creating a housing shortage of gigantic proportions and an economy of chronic scarcity that kept the Soviet population largely undernourished.[10] This sad state of affairs was dominated by a strictly centralized Soviet economic system, which preserved the inherent conservatism and inefficiency of the Stalinist mold—a kind of economic straitjacket with a built-in resistance to technological innovation, a rigid attitude which resulted in retaining enormous numbers of unskilled and unproductive manual jobs. This system was, furthermore, institutionalized through a cumbersome bureaucracy bent on fulfilling production quotas (even if nobody wanted to buy the shoddy goods), and when unable to meet these quotas, creating the illusion that they had succeeded.

While the world was being hoodwinked by the assertions of rapid gains by socialism, Brezhnev introduced the concept of "developed socialism"—a slogan duly embellished by the extensive network of propagandists extolling "the qualitative superiority of the socialist way of life."[11] However, the majority of Sovietologists failed to understand what was hidden behind the Soviet facade of "developed socialism"—a hollow euphemism, serving as a cover for ideological extravagance and Bolshevik incompetence in running a neo-Stalinist state. (Neo-Stalinism emerged after the fall of Khrushchev.)

A prominent Sovietologist summed up the four tendencies comprising a "developed socialist society" in the following manner:

> 1. *Economic*—a new economic system in accordance with the demands of the scientific-technical revolution, the harmonious development of the national economy, and an increase in the standard of living.
>
> 2. *Social*—the leading role of the working class, unity of the people, the continuation of the collective spirit, camaraderie and the socialist epoch.
>
> 3. *Political*—the scientific leadership of society through the Party, the development of the state system and socialist democracy, and
>
> 4. *Ideological*—the continuation of Marxism-Leninism, and the raising of the general educational level and professional knowledge.[12]

To be sure, these tendencies reflected the official Communist Party line, proclaiming the development of a socialist society, but what is surprising is that despite the onset of stagnation, Wolfgang Leonhard termed this shift as a move from a "socialist society" to a "developing socialist society" that marked the beginning of a "more realistic outlook . . . evident in all fields" with "the style of leadership changed from activist overoptimism into sober, bureaucratic realism."[13]

It is noteworthy that the secretive ideological tensions of unrealized goals escaped notice in Soviet studies—studies guided mostly by Western social science categories, in which the symptoms of Soviet structural decomposition were hidden behind a smokescreen of false pretenses that simply vanished in models of a conflict-free, self-regulating social system in which "the policy of relative equality of incomes and provision of extensive social welfare benefits has virtually eliminated poverty in the USSR."[14]

Furthermore, Western Sovietologists, strongly impressed by the fact that the Soviets managed to reconstruct and upgrade their military machine, gauged the strength of the Communist state in terms of the arms-control dialogue and the military competition with the United States, frequently overdramatized in the ambivalent concept of "peaceful coexistence." Still, the basic premises as well as the findings of Sovietologists represented a qualitatively poor enterprise by comparison with the highly sophisticated and intellectually powerful concepts employed by the leading students of international relations when speaking of arms control negotiations. These latter concepts included mutual assured destruction (MAD), mutual deterrence, limited wars, national security, and strategic bargaining—all in search of a formula for averting a nuclear catastrophe.[15]

Fascinated with impressions, images, and the posturing of the Soviet leaders, Sovietologists failed to evaluate correctly the boastful ideological claims of a classless and egalitarian ideal to be achieved in the near and radiant future—a claim which, in reality, obscured the fact that the Communists succeeded in building the ultimate "class" society, with tight social and political controls.

After evaluating the major works of Sovietologists for the last four decades,[16] the author of the essay "To the Stalin Mausoleum" concluded that contingent facticity, conceptual confusion, and overall misapprehension of seventy years of a "utopia in power" have been assiduously fostered by Western Sovietologists in an effort that "has done nothing to prepare us for the surprises of the past four years."[17] And indeed, despite a professed dedication to "the study of all matters that help us to understand the meaning of current, politically significant Soviet-communist behavior,"[18] a well-known Sovietologist, Alexander Motyl, offered the following comments as recently as the summer of 1989, which show us how confused and far off the mark some interpretations of Soviet political arrangements have been:

> Revolutions from above are preceded by conditions of multiple sovereignty, when radical and anti-radical forces within the state are engaged in a struggle for the upper hand. Revolutions from above may be said to have occurred when the radicals have won. . . . Given such a definition, it becomes immediately evident that the contemporary Soviet system is nowhere near a *critical condition* [emphasis added]. Agriculture and industry may be woefully inefficient and wasteful, the bureau-

cracy may be strangling society, youth may be disillusioned, and the ideology may have lost its appeal. In a word, the USSR's big problems may be—and obviously are—enormous and quite numerous. But as all scholars realize, there is no way to characterize the USSR's current condition as one of multiple sovereignty or anything even remotely approximating it; quite simply, genuine contenders are absent. The Baltic popular fronts, like the Armenian and Georgian movements, do not qualify, because in their very nature as the regionally focused nationalisms of peripherally located small nations, they represent limited, and therefore, fully containable "small problems."[19]

Surprisingly, a year later, forgetting his own sloppy exercise in the "scientific" interpretation of Soviet reality coupled with rather hasty predictions, this Soviet specialist entered into a substantive discussion centered on the sorry state of Western Sovietology, stating that "contemporary Sovietology represents an awkward amalgam of data collection, policy analysis, and journalism that is divorced from scholarship as sense impressions are from theory."[20]

What is of significance in Motyl's statement is that his indictment of Sovietology constituted a new awareness of the many deficiencies in the field, although his criticism was of a limited nature, lacking a clearly defined mode of explaining the detrimental influence of the correlated defects. To highlight this criticism more fully, we must address ourselves to the deeper-lying causes of the failures of Sovietology, which are related to decades of research and practice in the discipline. It is these pervasive causes that greatly contributed to the many misperceptions in the analysis of the Soviet political system. The misreading of Soviet reality in the West unfolded the aggregate of conceptual confusion, based on disingenuous observations and leading to mistaken assumptions about a radical restructuring of Soviet post-Stalinist society.

It is with the simple, basic relation of two kinds of knowledge—namely, the "inauthentic" which circumvents the truth of reality, and the "authentic" which confronts it—that Z., the author of the essay "To the Stalin Mausoleum," defined the major causes that contributed to the derailment of Western Sovietology. Z. formulated the emergence of stubborn fallacies that haunted the discipline in this way:

> It is precisely because during the past twenty-odd years mainline Western Sovietology has concentrated on the sources of Soviet "stability" as a "mature industrial society" with a potential for "pluralist development" that it has prepared us so poorly for the present crisis, not only in the Soviet Union but in communist systems everywhere. Instead of taking the Soviet leadership at its ideological word—that their task was

to "build socialism"—Western Sovietology has by and large foisted on Soviet reality social science categories derived from Western realities, with the result that the extraordinary, indeed surreal, Soviet experience has been rendered banal to the point of triviality.[21]

In retrospect, this unfortunate state of affairs, which dates back to the 1960s, had its start with the declared obsolescence of the totalitarian model because, according to one "authority" on the Soviet Union, the model "inflated partial insights into full axiomatic truths," translated into an "elliptical narrative, bogus analysis, and pseudointerpretation."[22] This was—from both the theoretical and the realistic standpoints—a drastic step in a direction that utterly disregarded the oppressive, neo-Stalinist character of the Soviet state. Furthermore, Sovietologists claimed that the application of the authoritarian label to the Soviet system was allegedly more timely and more fitting to the emerging, more tolerant social order of the Communist state. Refusing to acknowledge the totalitarian, neo-Stalinist character of the Soviet state, Western Sovietologists neglected Soviet literature that was dedicated to the assault on the integrity of the individual—part of a game plan to control the development of the "new" Soviet man in the overall effort to manage and control in a "scientific" manner Soviet society (see Chapter 4). In the attempt to reintegrate the Soviet system into the normative patterns of Western social science, Sovietologists misinterpreted the overbearing and deadening features of the Brezhnev-Podgorny-Kosygin era and, despite indications to the contrary, bestowed on it a measure of stability and a modicum of normalcy. Thus, the respectability and maturity of the Soviet social order finally found its place in the untidy and malleable context of the authoritarian model.

This change of direction in Soviet studies, reflecting the extensive use of Western social science categories, was gradual and uneven. However, the process accelerated with the publication in 1969 of a highly influential book with the impressive title *Communist Studies and the Social Sciences*.[23] The general purpose of this work was explained by one of the major contributors, Erik P. Hoffman, a prominent Sovietologist in his own right, who declared in his essay "Communication Theory and the Study of Soviet Politics":

> We can and we must make greater use of the generalizations contained in the growing social science literature. The propositions that comprise various theories (e.g., communication theory, organization theory, role theory) can be very useful in generating new hypotheses, raising im-

portant questions, and discovering data available but hitherto untapped. Furthermore, it is high time that Soviet specialists make a concerted effort to contribute to this literature.[24]

Of course, this kind of advice cannot be fully understood without undertaking a brief analysis of the serious and frequently controversial methodological problems that arise in connection with the variability and instability of social phenomena. This quandary of the social sciences is best explained in terms of Thomas S. Kuhn's observation that no paradigm is capable of explaining all in the world that needs to be explained.[25] Nonetheless, political scientists are inclined to disregard this dictum, displaying a paradigmatic view of reality even if it is knowledge of a limited and abstract quality. In this struggle to maintain a paradigm, three approaches dominate the field of political science:

1. *Structural Functionalism*: This approach is generally judged unsatisfactory in explaining the nature and workings of social systems because of its ethnocentrism, with its theoretical emphasis on stability and resistance to change in the context of Anglo-American norms and political traditions.

2. *The Development Theory*: Gabriel Almond and James Coleman, editors of the influential *The Politics of Developing Areas*, sought to discern universal functions and processes, but Almond and Coleman acknowledged that the questions raised in the volume were "based on the distinctive political activities existing in Western complex systems."[26] For example, they enumerate three "output functions" of political systems—1. Rule-making. 2. Rule application. 3. Rule adjudication" (p17)—without even mentioning that these functions are only a still more abstract rendering of the already somewhat abstract American idea of the "separation of powers." Assessing the writings of other prominent developmentalists (including Eisenstadt and Kautsky), one critic observed that "too much research in this field involved a reckless sort of data collection, variable definition, operationalization, and statistical manipulation without benefit of theory."[27]

3. *Pluralism*: The proponents of pluralism focus on diverse interest groups, conflict, and questions of political power. However, the concept of power is vaguely or narrowly defined. As one critic argued, "one thesis of the present critique of the pluralists is that they *do not have* a rich theory, and continually push the burden of their methodological problems from one part of their theory to another."[28]

It is not surprising that the noted political scientist Peter Rutland, discussing the failings of Sovietology, declared:

Sovietology is not an aberrant case but is symptomatic of a general crisis besetting the social sciences. Unfortunately, there is no agreed framework for explanation in the social sciences.[29]

In addition to these methodological and theoretical problems, the fact that social processes vary with institutional settings limits the synthesizing perspective of the political science theories that cut across the political-cultural differences between the democratic West and the Communist Soviet state. Undeterred by these differences—differences that presented formidable difficulties—another trendsetter, *The Behavioral Revolution in Communist Studies*,[30] made its appearance in 1971. Paying tribute to the great achievements of modern social and behavioral sciences, one of the major contributors to this work called on Sovietologists for an "increased focus in political science on observable actions of individuals and groups, as opposed to a concentration on constitutional and legal questions."[31]

Thus the behaviorist trend in Sovietology grew out of the influence of a social science fad, out of what we might call a "methodological revolution" based on the assimilation of alien theoretical material, which frequently absolved itself from empirical scrutiny when larger numbers of relevant variables escaped the process of verification. With normative propositions to be avoided (according to the behavioral creed, moral judgments are the result of subjective preferences lacking universal or objective validity), the emphasis was narrowed down to the development of generalizations that offered explanations or predictions about political behavior in the context of descriptive statements restricted to a relatively limited range of evidence and logic. For proponents of this methodological revolution, the political content was not simply expressed in linguistic elucidation; it was, above all, a demand for a scientific approach corresponding to accepted canons of observational procedures in the study of behavior of individual persons or small groups. This application of scientific observational procedures was not "likely to focus on ideologies, constitutions or laws or upon the organizational structure of institutions," but diverted its attention instead to "studies of characteristics of decision makers and of factors influencing decision making."[32]

The common objection to this methodological revolution, usually designated as behavioristic or positivistic, is that it cannot take into account what people feel or think in terms of motives or goals. Like all other knowledge, this approach is usually premised on the basis of objective signs that are not readily verified—a condition exacerbated by difficulties in gathering ascertainable data or facts on the Soviet Union. This is one of the reasons why the behavioral approach did not succeed in detecting the aberrant trends of neo-Stalinism and their corroding impact on Soviet society.

Actually, Western Sovietologists developed a pattern of intellectual pride—a sort of insensitivity to Soviet real life and politics—that confused in the methodological context what is and what is not empirical and failed to take into consideration the pervasive features of the totalitarian-bureaucratic system of the Soviet state. Thus, in search of more "objective" knowledge, some Sovietologists attempted to explain Soviet experience in terms of a dynamic model of modernization, even going so far as to assume that once two countries develop heavy industries capable of producing super-weapons, the two systems will converge, evolving in the process similar major institutions, similar traditions, and eventually a similar style of life.[33] It is remarkable that not only Sovietologists succumbed to this "sophisticated" prognosis. The prominent economist John Kenneth Galbraith visited the Soviet Union in 1984—at the nadir of the Soviet economy's stagnation—and, on his return, emphasized in one of his books that the similarities between the two systems would lead to their convergence, because

> the Soviet economy has made great material progress in recent years . . . [as] is evident both from statistics . . . and from the general urban scene. . . . Partly the Russian system succeeds because, in contrast with the Western industrial economies, it makes full use of its manpower.[34]

The rather inauspicious "theory of convergence" was followed by assertions that the Soviet Union under Brezhnev reached a liberalizing if not benign state and that the imperatives of industrialization and modernization created the favorable conditions for the model of "institutional pluralism" sometimes interchangeable with "bureaucratic pluralism." A representative of this school claimed that

> the Soviet political system really features numerous complexes and subcomplexes that cut across the formal institutions. (The word *complex* is being used as it is in the phrase "military industrial complex," to denote officials in different institutions who have similar enough interests to form an important political group.) The complexes include not only the party and government officials with similar backgrounds and functional responsibilities, but the specialized officials of Gosplan, the trade unions, the Young Communist League, and so on.[35]

Such "informal" aspects of Soviet life were important, although falling short of genuine pluralism. These aspects of the Soviet regime were strengthened, of course, by Mikhail Gorbachev's *perestroika*, which was often identified with the emergence of "civil society."[36] Despite the claims of some social scientists, "civil society" was rudimentary at best before Gorbachev, and even the impact of Gorbachev's reforms was probably overpraised.

The pluralistic characterization of Soviet society, featuring structural and functional differentiation among "numerous complexes and subcomplexes" whose partitioning lines were blurred, did not begin to reflect Soviet reality. A more accurate portrayal of the neo-Stalinist society—one portrayal that did not pretend to discover social divisions behind the implied special interests—was offered by a more astute observer of the Soviet scene, Vladimir Shlapentokh:

> The majority of the dominant class consists of the apparatchiks, who implement the dictates of the political elite. . . . The political elite in Soviet society holds a monopoly on strategic decisions—those decisions that generate or block any significant change in social life—*and expends considerable energy attempting to prevent the emergence of any competing center of power.*[37]

And indeed, when we critically scrutinize recent Soviet history before the Gorbachev era, it is obvious that the "methodological revolution" offered precious little insight into the workings of the neo-Stalinist state with its flourishing climate of intimidation, cynical corruption, and the general deterioration of values, rightfully described by the Polish essayist Adam Michnik as a "totalitarianism with its teeth knocked out."[38] This failure to view Soviet reality from the totalitarian-bureaucratic perspective contributed greatly to an assessment of Soviet society as a multifaceted community geared to a common future—an assertion based more on wishful thinking than on questioning appearances as *appearances*. This fallacy is particularly prevalent in Western studies of the Soviet electoral system. Thus, one Sovietologist declared that "elections in the USSR are symbolic displays of social unity and consensus. The structure of the electoral campaign and the voting process reflect this ritualistic function."[39] In another example, the Sovietologist Theodore H. Friedgut states:

> Soviet electoral politics, though abounding in phenomena that indicate great potential for adding authoritative dimensions to voters' preferences, are as yet largely symbolic and socializing in their function. . . . There appear to exist pressures in the Soviet Union for movement into a stage of adaptation in which detailed, all-embracing Party control and the centralizing monopoly on political power would give way to a more balanced distribution of forces composed of functional groups,

intellectual critics, and participating citizens, all exercising some initiative in the determination of social priorities within an overall framework of Communist power. . . . Such changes are as yet nowhere visible. In the meantime we find the social and governmental institutions of the Soviet Union caught between a transformation of society in which citizens are mobilized to protect the dominance of authority, and a consolidation in which revolutionary fervor has waned and the Party rules through bureaucratic *fiat*, tempered only slightly by the pressures of economic and social modernization.[40]

Evidently, despite the vaguely implied "pressures," the party's "centralized monopoly on political power" was not altered by universal suffrage and the 99 percent voter turnout. Before 1987, Soviet elections did not represent a political contest in Western terms. The elections, on all levels, were treated more as a festival, carefully orchestrated by apparatchiks, with actual balloting playing a minor role. Interestingly, among reasons Friedgut noted for the high turnout of voters is that "while no person interviewed was able to cite a case of any sanctions being employed against someone who failed to vote, there was general consensus that a refusal to vote out of simple political passivity would be noted somewhere and could at some point in the future cause unpleasantness to the nonvoter."[41]

For a more revealing item attesting to the long arm of the party, Friedgut cites the case of a candidate who was shouted down by the people, who refused to confirm his candidacy. The party yielded and endorsed another candidate, one favored by the people (this is an extraordinary incident, because, as a rule, the Soviet electorate was characteristically passive and docile). However, the party promoted the unpopular candidate to a higher Soviet function, while on a fabricated pretext, the candidate favored by the people was expelled from the party and assigned to a harder, less-skilled job.[42]

In contrast to the more friendly Sovietologists, Zbigniew Brzezinski and Samuel Huntington categorically declared that popular participation in the Soviet Union was vastly different from that in democratic countries. In fact, they stated, "the Soviet regime increasingly uses political participation to control its people [and] the controls produced by political participation flow in one direction only."[43] This realistic observation puts to rest any attempt to elevate Soviet elections to a "symbolic display of social unity and consensus."

Genuine cognitive value can be claimed only if what is directly or indirectly observed is usually expressed in terms that relate closely to the materials of conceptualized experience. It is from this perspective that the behavioral approach ended in failure, incapable of doing justice to Soviet actuality which was perceived in a body of knowledge dedicated largely to an "anomaly-reducing" enterprise. As Erik P. Hoffman summarized it:

> The Communist area specialist may have much to *contribute* to, and much to *gain* from, social science theory. Particularly important are theories and hypotheses of a "puzzle-solving" or an anomaly-reducing nature.[44]

The attempt to picture the Soviet Union as a "normal" and "stable" entity led to efforts designed to remove the anomalies of Soviet experience—a form of political theorizing dedicated to turning the totalitarian into an authoritarian model. An example of a sanitized 1983 version of the Soviet system, by a Sovietologist who refused to apply the totalitarian label, follows:

> Above all, the Soviet leadership and political elite clearly have the will to rule the Soviet Union and the Soviet empire by traditional means, and also expand Soviet influence and power globally, to benefit from the decades of sacrifices and development. In the equation of foreign policies of opposing powers, the capacity to act and the will to act are partly exchangeable; the greater will to act may overcome the shortcomings of a nation's capacities. . . . What has been built through generations with much blood, sacrifices, ruthlessness, cunning, and conviction, *will not simply disintegrate or radically change because of critical problems.* In the coming succession, the Soviet Union may face a leadership crisis and an economic crisis, but it does not now and in all probability will not in the next decade face a systemic crisis that endangers its existence. It has enormous unused reserves of political and social stability. Gigantic economies such as the Soviet Union's, presided by intelligent and educated professionals, do not go bankrupt. They become less effective, stagnate or experience an absolute decline for a period, but they do not disintegrate.[45]

It is rather strange, but in his book *The Soviet Paradox*, published four years later—after Gorbachev publicly acknowledged the severity of the Soviet crisis, calling for a profound transformation of the economy—Severyn Bialer still maintained that "the (Soviet) system would not crumble, the political situation would not disintegrate, the economy would not go bankrupt, the leadership would not lose its will to rule internally or its will to be a global power."[46] Apparently, Bialer—compelled to move from the real to the ideal—did not take into consideration de Tocqueville's dictum that "the most dangerous time for a bad government is when it starts to reform itself."[47]

Justifiably, the discipline of Sovietology experienced some scattered countertendencies and not all Sovietologists succumbed to the blandishments of the methodological revolution. It is true that no one can claim credit for predicting the spectacular collapse of the Soviet empire, but Richard Pipes of Harvard University, Robert Conquest of the Hoover Institute, Zbigniew Brzezinski of the Center for Strategic Studies, and Marshall J. Goldman, generally recognized as the foremost authority on the Soviet economy, were among the most persistent critics of the Soviet regime, stressing its corrupt and oppressive character. Similarly, while sharing the view of Soviet modernization, Stanley Rothman and George W. Breslauer displayed a measure of scholarly objectivity in assessing the structural and functional character of the Soviet system:

> Thus, as in the West, modernization in the U.S.S.R. has led to structural and functional differentiation, which has been reflected in separate institutions charged with administrative, executive, and legislative functions. Unlike the Western pattern of modernization, however, Communist Party rule has been consciously superimposed on this institutional development, in order to prevent such differentiation from leading to a government based upon genuine separation of powers, checks and balances, and liberal democratic values.[48]

Another notable scholar who understood the extent of brutal state power of the Soviet regime was Adam B. Ulam, the author of an authoritative biography of Stalin[49] and other preeminent studies of the Communist state. In 1976 Adam B. Ulam counseled Western Sovietologists that they should dedicate themselves to careful and intensive scholarship free of ideological preconceptions, urging them to moderate their "passion for abstract models and methodology" and not to "neglect the living reality of a hugely important and interesting political system."[50]

Reviewing the body of evidence in major works on the Soviet Union produced over the last four decades, one must conclude that Ulam's appeal for objective and insightful scholarship went unheeded. In the attempt to illuminate common patterns of behavior across dissimilar political cultures, the great majority of Western Sovietologists scaled the "ladder of abstraction,"[51] violating one of the basic principles of inquiry neatly formulated by Thomas S. Kuhn: "Assimilating a new sort of fact demands a more than additive adjustment of theory, and until that adjustment is completed—until the scientist has learned to see nature [in our case social and governmental structures] in a different way—the new fact is not quite a fact."[52]

Kuhn's principle of inquiry explains in highly instructive terms the ineptitude of some scholars in the field of Sovietology, who did not produce a workable description of Soviet reality but subjected Soviet phenomena to definite theoretical presuppositions interpreted according to a mechanistic transfer of Western social science categories. This lack of understanding of the sources and depth of the insoluble difficulties besetting the Soviet system may best be exemplified in George W. Breslauer's excerpt from Jerry Hough's articles, which were written about Brzezinski's analysis of the Brezhnev regime. According to Breslauer, Hough has emphasized

> the existence of societal supports for the Soviet system in the past and trends since 1964 which he argues would be likely to increase support for the Soviet regime among key social and political groups; movement toward "institutional pluralism," greater functional autonomy from Party prescription, *diminished emphasis on dogma*, expanded specialist and mass input into decision-making processes, incremental improvements in consumer welfare, an end to "revolutions from above," an egalitarian social policy, and a general war on poverty in town [and] especially countryside.[53]

It seems that George Orwell anticipated in 1945 the jargon of the comfortable professor defending Soviet totalitarianism:

> While freely conceding that the Soviet regime exhibits certain features which the humanitarian may be inclined to deplore, we must, I think, agree that a certain curtailment of the right to political opposition is an unavoidable concomitant of transitional periods, and that the rigors which the Russian people have been called upon to undergo have been amply justified in the sphere of concrete achievements.[54]

The conspicuous indifference to Communist categories of thought, coupled with the almost universal disinclination to develop a viable theoretical model of the Soviet bureaucratic totalitarianism, turned the bulk of Sovietology into a pseudo-science, incapable of a scholarly analysis of the Soviet system. This mindset or wish to consign to oblivion the totalitarian model was clearly stated by a prominent political scientist: "If neglected with sufficient vigor," it is quite possible that "the totalitarian construct will be overtaken, if not by oblivion, at least by creeping desuetude."[55]

An equally strange but highly original explanation for the demise of the totalitarian model—albeit inspired by the cure-all properties of the modernization process—was offered in 1980 by the renowned writer and essayist Michael Walzer:

> Totalitarianism, with the purges, can be conceived as "disease" to which nations are peculiarly susceptible during the crisis period—a view that

justifies efforts to prevent the disease and has therefore been favored by American writers. . . . At the same time, however . . . the future of Soviet society is somehow not a problem—only the past is a problem: the modernizing process will go on; the disease of Stalinism will be shaken off and the patient brought to a condition that, it is assumed, will be healthy simply because it will be modern.[56]

Here, the modernization process, regardless of the sharp tensions between its scientific and political aspects, extends a promise of a future healthy condition—a questionable conjecture, to say the least, and a topic that would take us far from our area of inquiry. Instead, we shall focus on the attempt to use the term "disease" as a substantial definition of totalitarianism. Undoubtedly, Soviet totalitarianism under Stalin—also known as "barrack socialism"[57]—displayed many features that may be classified as a social disease, as a pathology of the social fabric, with its widespread terror, purges, and man-made famines. Largely ignored was the fact that the strong reemergence of neo-Stalinism, subdued for a short span during the "thaw," preserved these pathological symptoms in a new totalitarian-bureaucratic setting. As Leszek Kolakowski observed, the Soviet people, oppressed by the arbitrary dictatorship of the party, experienced "overall nationalization of everything, including *people's minds, historical knowledge, every means of communication [and] all human relationships.*"[58]

In even stronger terms, the writer-dissident Tarsis also discerned adverse modifications in the personal, social, and moral make-up of *Homo Sovieticus*:

[He] lost any notion of what the people round him meant by good, evil, morality, convictions, belief; it seemed to him that for a long time none of all these things had existed in his country. . . . It was also difficult for him to judge his own life and actions. Living was thus unspeakably hard and painful for him. . . . Words had ceased to have any resonance, they had no force, they rustled like dry fallen leaves—a sort of lifeless garbage.[59]

Thus, under neo-Stalinism, whether based on enforced consensus or on other modes of ideological persuasion, the Soviet person was forced to abandon part of his or her humanity and, unable to resist the strong personality-oriented pressures, submitted to the central organizational power, the state—a state that intermittently has waged war on its citizens.

This psychological profile of the Soviet man drawn by Tarsis—a profile completely missed by Sovietologists—is a perfect example of the way in which Marxism-Leninism was "socializing humanity." As one keen observer of the Soviet scene noted, this persistent ideological pressure went even "further in the promotion of obsessions"—it "tried to make man *possessed*; the object—the absolute possession of men."[60]

Even so, Communist society was not only formed along consciousness levels grounded in exclusionary claims to power; it was also founded on material, institutional, and pseudo-democratic levels. Hence, the bureaucratic-totalitarian model is a genuine reflection of all the levels of the monopolistic, post-Stalinist power structure and is clearly a visible construct, taking into consideration the political and social dimensions of Marxism-Leninism. Only with this approach are we capable of addressing the problems of Soviet rule, which were based on the "built-in tendency to regulate all realms of human activity."[61] As the author of "To the Stalin Mausoleum" stated:

> Totalitarianism does not mean that such regimes in fact exercise total control over the population; it means rather that such control is their aspiration. It does not mean they are omnipotent in performance, but instead that they are institutionally omnicompetent. It is not Soviet society that is totalitarian, but the Soviet state.[62]

Let us add here that the definition of Soviet totalitarianism in terms of a pathological syndrome implies "behavior" or "actions that are destructive of group or individual integrity," leading to a "malaise in the sense of an assault, unsought or deliberate, on social wholeness."[63] At the root of this assault is a fundamental difference in attitude toward political life—a political life subjected to Marxist-Leninist strictures, which were geared to a distant future of dreamlike projections tailored to the vague fancies of the common man.

If we are emphatic in the retention of the totalitarian model in a bureaucratic setting, we must, first of all, dispense with the problem of its adaptability to the post-Stalinist Soviet state.

As is generally known, according to the logic of preference and the logic of justification, the theoreticians of the Stalinist model of totalitarianism established a common underlying pattern of six interrelated traits: an ideology; a single mass party headed by a leader; a secret, terroristic police; a monopoly of all means of communication; a monopoly of weapons; and a centrally planned economy.[64] While these traits have been explored at length in the annals of Sovietology, it should be kept in mind that they have been selected in a one-sidedly critical approach, construed as a comprehensive assessment of the totalitarian model. Some prominent Sovietologists attempted to correct the imbalance, adding a modest number of properties to the model, such as "the subversion of independent associations and loci of power," "the mobilization of affect," "the institutionalization of anxiety"—all classified under the heading of a "totalitarian mystique."[65]

Still, even with the additional derivatives of the model, the attempt to explain major building blocks of Stalinism exerted a constraining effect on Sovietology, particularly after Stalin's demise when the totalitarian model, at least in the view of Western Sovietologists, lost its criteria of reference. More centrally, the refusal to devote research and attention to the utility of totalitarian traits germane to the few decades of neo-Stalinism generated misleading substantive implications which were expressed in deficient explanations of Soviet reality. Consigning the totalitarian model to the role of an historical anomaly of the past, Western Sovietologists enshrined the permanent six traits of the totalitarian model as features of a structurally unique system, symbolizing only the high marks of Stalinist rule.[66]

What Sovietologists failed to realize is that the original six traits of Communist totalitarianism represented only the *vertical* properties of the Stalinist mode—properties that, with some variations, could serve as a truthful description of the post-Stalinist period. In other words, these properties take on an explicit meaning as vertical *functional* concepts that reflect only the rigid centralization of a Soviet state administration geared to ensure decisive party involvement in all spheres of political, social, and economic life of the country. This involvement of party hierarchy in vital areas included, just to name a few, ensuring that ministerial directives and, above all, party resolutions were put into effect; establishing limits and controlling functions among different levels of government; restricting and controlling agricultural labor in the collectives; and managing the intricate system of *nomenklatura,* designed to promote able or ideologically reliable party members to political, industrial, and national posts.

By contrast, *horizontal* concepts, in their broad meaning, have to do with goals-means relationships in shaping and reshaping society and history—an enterprise accomplished with the imposition and promotion of an official ideology, which was reinforced with a censorship mechanism aimed at controlling the content of mass communications and public expression. In a more detailed approach (based on the foregoing) horizontal concepts help us to identify the more specific goals and means of the Soviet Communist Party, such as the promulgation of the Marxist shibboleth known as the unity of theory and practice, the distorted version of democratic principles, the control of human behavior and development, and the propagation of Marxist-Leninist philosophy.

The chief advantage of employing horizontal and vertical concepts is that the confluence of both will facilitate the analysis of complex issues and will subject certain long-standing assumptions to reappraisal. But first let us explore the background and the nature of the vertical concepts in the context of neo-Stalinism.

George Orwell's *1984*—one of the most important documents of our century—was first published in 1949.[67] At that time, the phenomenon of totalitarianism was already the subject of heated polemics, and it had been so ever since Franz Neumann introduced the term into the social sciences prior to World War II.[68] However, it is noteworthy that Orwell's work also served, in a sense, as a forerunner of a great number of competent theoretical studies on totalitarianism in the early and mid-1950s, as if their authors had intended to develop and improve on Emanuel Goldstein's "Theory and Practice of Oligarchical Collectivism" in *1984*.[69] Thus, for example, Hannah Arendt's *Origins of Totalitarianism* was published in 1951, Czeslav Milosz's *The Captive Mind* appeared in 1953, and Zbigniew K. Brzezinski's *The Permanent Purge: Politics in Soviet Totalitarianism* came out in 1956.

By comparison, one of the more serious attempts to understand the nature and the workings of a totalitarian regime was marked by the appearance, in 1956, of *Totalitarian Dictatorship and Autocracy*,[70] a collaborative effort of Zbigniew K. Brzezinski and Carl J. Friedrich. This work quickly established itself as the most influential version of the concept of totalitarianism for the next decade.

In 1965, Friedrich, who co-authored the study, found it imperative to prepare a new and revised edition of *Totalitarian Dictatorship and Autocracy*[71] because of "numerous developments in the practice of totalitarian dictatorship . . . greatly increased documentation of past activities, and . . . vigorous discussion concerning the nature of this form of government."[72] However, despite Friedrich's addition of some new chapters to this revision, his revamped version of the totalitarian state remained essentially the same as the original model set forth in the 1956 publication: that is, the conceptual focal point was defined as the totalitarian "syndrome"—presumably with the hidden assumption of a pathological despotism—and again was characterized by a pattern of interrelated basic features comprising an official ideology, a single mass party led by one individual, a system of terror on a mass scale, monopolies on communications and weapons, and a centrally directed and planned economy.[73]

However, from the standpoint of comparative politics, some of the conceptual categorizations of the "six traits cluster" are subject to challenge. For example, it is not difficult to criticize Friedrich and Brzezinski's definition of the role of ideology as "an official body of doctrine covering all aspects of man's existence to which everyone living in that society is supposed to adhere."[74] First of all, the authors failed to point out that the very term "ideology" has a double—and quite contradictory—meaning in the Soviet political lexicon.

In one sense, ideology in the Soviet Union was considered a conglomeration of false rationalizations of the bourgeois ruling classes, used for the purpose of justifying and preserving the political and economic relations of capitalist society. But in another sense, the use of the term "ideology" related to an entire system of ideas applied to the interpretation of Soviet experience—a system that was manifested in a total commitment to the practices and institutions of the Communist Party. In other words, in this second sense, the official Soviet ideology was an embodiment of views and ideas imposed as the political and social determinant of knowledge and propagated with the intent of inculcating unshakable beliefs—requiring no justification and permitting no questions. This was the kind of ideology which, according to Friedrich and Brzezinski, constituted "an operative force in totalitarian political orders."[75] However, this "operative force," with its official body of doctrine, was relevant only to Stalinist Russia and hardly could fit into the concept of ideology promulgated in Hitler's Germany or Mussolini's Italy. Any attempt to consider this brand of ideology as either an intellectual construct or an identifying catch-all feature of totalitarian regimes overlooks a very important fact: fascist ideologies, highly extravagant and given to disproportionate exaggerations, are outspokenly anti-intellectual. To be sure, Friedrich and Brzezinski spoke at length about the role of myths in fascist ideologies. But quite significantly, the word "fascism" means nothing more than a "combat-group" ideology—glorifying the animating force of life, its primitive drives, and the "call of blood" (whatever *that* means!) but lacking in any commitment to the very intellectual concept able to inspire a genuine revolutionary movement.

By contrast, Friedrich and Brzezinski were correct in their analysis of the officially imposed ideological "truths'" as the driving force of a promised utopia in the distant future, while the existing social order would eventually dissolve itself into the ideal millenium—be it the Communist classless society, the Thousand Year Reich, or the Roman Empire restored in all its splendor and glory.

Obviously, under any totalitarian regime, concepts, words, and values are stripped of their traditional meanings, and moral standards are radically distorted. But in the former Soviet Union, the Communist Party was equally determined to exert a controlling influence over *all* aspects of the moral upbringing of the "new Soviet man." Consequently, Soviet ethical literature was heavily infused with Marxist-Leninist precepts, emphasized as the highest human ideals, to be realized in the process of a "necessary, natural, and historically long period in the form of the Communist system."[76] Accordingly, one of the leading Soviet ethicists, A. I. Titarenko, elevated to the highest moral principles the following "values":

1. Devotion to the ideal of communism.
2. Conscientious, honest, and selfless labor dedicated to the building of socialism and communism.
3. Collectivism and group solidarity as necessary forms of social development—a major requirement in streamlining the socialist economy.[77]

Thus the Communist Party itself set the general framework concerning the central image of man, so that all that was left for Soviet ethicists, in deference to their ideological elders, was simply to fill in the necessary details. This enterprise paved the way for the indoctrination process of *collective responsibility*—a type of responsibility experienced by every Soviet citizen at any stage of his or her life. In fact, the role of the collective appeared to be one of the most durable features of Soviet political culture[78] and served as an instrument for social control—a feature quite frequently ignored[79] by writers studying Communist regimes in the context of the totalitarian model.

With due allowance for these shortcomings, Brzezinski and Friedrich's theoretical construct was nevertheless a credible descriptive framework for the workings of a totalitarian regime. The emphasis on indoctrination and political mobilization of the masses, the extraordinary sense of purpose and dedication of the single-party apparatus, the role of the dictator, and the use of terror as an integral part of the systemic effort to control every aspect of social and intellectual life—these were the *tour de force* highlights of a totalitarian dictatorship.

While this version of the totalitarian model is quite attractive as a way of explaining the nature of Stalinist Russia, it is of questionable efficacy regarding the workings of the political system in the now-defunct Soviet Union after Stalin's death. This is perhaps why the early and middle sixties witnessed a virtual flood of political science literature, which not only criticized the limitations of the totalitarian model but also represented an attempt to reassess and explain the new state-power-society relationship in post-Stalinist Russia. Out of this plethora of descriptive, abstract images of social phenomena in the Soviet Union emerged a number of clarifying explanations (and not-so-clarifying comments, because of a lack of empirical evidence) under the headings of an oligarchic model, a "modernization" model, an imperial model, a developmental model, and even an institutional-pluralistic model. Still, one of the more valuable and quite promising additions in this attempt to understand the workings of the former Soviet state system was undoubtedly the bureaucratic model.

Based on the Weberian and post-Weberian theoretical studies, the bureaucratic model faithfully reflected the elimination of terror and arbitrary cruelty on a mass scale (although these still persisted in some areas of Soviet life, as in the treatment of dissidents and "refuseniks") as well as indicated in a "subtle shift from personal dictatorship to institutional or bureaucratic authority."[80] With the introduction of the bureaucratic model[81] came new descriptive terms, supposedly reflecting the workings of modern Communist societies: "totalitarianism without terror," "the administered society," and the not very ingenious "rationalization of party control."

Still, the image of a Soviet bureaucracy—staffed by technocrats who professed diverse values and goals and generated alternative policies based on technical and rational criteria—was highly misleading. The Soviet Union could not be understood "as a giant bureaucracy, something like a modern corporation extended over the entire society, or a 'General Motors writ large'."[82] Of course, Friedrich and Brzezinski are correct in observing that "totalitarianism . . . is paralleled by a steady expansion of bureaucracy and bureaucratization."[83] However, they also pointed to the supremacy of the party, which represented "parallel governmental and party bureaucracies,"[84] a view that in some degree underestimated the role of the party.

The chief elements in the Soviet bureaucratic model were parochial priorities expressed in a set of routines established not so much by tradition as by the authority of the state through rigidly imposed modes of communication. Since the public sector in the Soviet Union was all-encompassing and every factory, store, or institution was owned and run by the state, the authors of the model listed four major groups representing Soviet bureaucracy: (1) the party apparatus, the so-called *apparatchiki*; (2) the professional military; (3) the state bureaucracy; and (4) the technical and economic bureaucracy. The task of coordinating and controlling this huge public sector with its inherent compartmentalized bureaucracy—even in conditions of overcentralization—was quite enormous and was literally inconceivable with-out the commanding role of the Communist Party. To be sure, the bureaucratic process in the former Soviet Union displayed a dynamic of its own, which in some respects will be familiar to students of administrative systems in the West. However, the absence of extra-administrative restraints, the absence of a civil service, and the lack of serious legal traditions—taken together with the Soviet bureaucratic imperative never to admit mistakes—allowed for a frequent abuse of power and privilege, to the distinct disadvantage of the average citizen.

Apart from underrating the Communist Party leadership or, at best, placing it on a par with other administrative groups in the former Soviet Union, the bureaucratic model overlooked the confusion and the proverbial inefficiency of Soviet officialdom. Moreover, concentrating in great measure on the administrative functions of the bureaucracy, this model was hardly an answer to the question of long-range policies and the manner in which they were determined. In a sense, this represents the greatest weakness of the model, particularly since we are left in the dark about the origin and the process of high-level policymaking—due, no doubt, to a lack of empirical evidence. In addition, the model only implied a certain lack of independence on the part of Soviet bureaucracy to challenge openly the basic assumptions underlying the tactics and strategies of policymaking.

Most scholars agree that the totalitarian model is no longer an accurate representation of the post-Stalinist political system. However, this theoretical inadequacy can be surmounted in a synthesis of the totalitarian and the bureaucratic models, since—at least in some respects—the now-defunct Soviet Union retained totalitarian techniques uniquely adapted to the assertion of its power in the modern world.

This crossbred synthesis, easily adaptable to the decades of neo-Stalinism, may be sketched in the following framework:

1. Soviet Communism was monolithic in nature, and faith in the Marxist-Leninist ideology was a major unifying factor of Soviet society. As Leszek Kolakowski observed, "The Soviet system could not do without this ideology, which (was) the sole *raison d'etre* for the existing apparatus of power."[85] However, with the growing discrepancy between promise and the *de facto* performance of the regime, Marxist-Leninist ideology *per se* ceased to be central to Soviet decisions, particularly in the area of foreign affairs, although it remained a "bridge"[86] that Soviet officials and Soviet citizens were compelled to cross.

2. The Soviet Communist Party—a party apparatus in every respect

the personification of a collective Machiavellian Prince, organized as it was along the lines of strict discipline—was instilled with a deep-seated[87] ideological commitment and a propensity for action inspired by an all-embracing political philosophy of absolute certainty. It was a party that felt assured of future power and considered every other political entity as a rival and an obstacle to the fulfillment of its "historical" mission. Because it controlled all the levers and springs of action, the party was either *superior* to the government bureaucracy or an inseparable part of it.

3. While a system of terror was a matter of the Stalinist past, a leading analyst of the Soviet political system argued correctly that "every totalitarian regime makes some place for terror in its system of controls—an awareness of its potentialities *conditions* the behavior of the totalitarian subject."[88]

And indeed, with the shift from mass-scale repressions and widespread executions, the state's coercive instruments were retained and even strengthened under Brezhnev and Andropov, when the Soviet regime attempted to prevent and punish unorthodox political behavior of dissidents. "Different-mindedness" was punished not only by intimidation, blackmail, and manipulation but also with lengthy incarceration, exile, or confinement to special psychiatric hospitals.[89]

4. To impose an official ideology, a huge bureaucracy controlled by the party reserved for the state a nearly complete monopoly over all means of persuasion including the communications media, such as the press, radio, television, and motion pictures. In the pre-Gorbachev era, with the exception of the sporadic, underground *Samizdat* literature, all book and newspaper publishing was in the hands of the state, and there was little likelihood that any written material that did not conform to the officially imposed ideology would ever see the light of day.

5. The entire Soviet economy, including the centralization of economic planning, was subject to the control of the state. In most vital areas, the Soviet economy was still in the grip of the Stalinist economic model, which was anything but responsive to consumer needs or sophisticated industrial requirements (examples include collectivization, cotton monoculture, and the defense industry).

6. Conditioning the Soviet individual to subordinate himself or herself to the will of the majority in the name of collectivist responsibility and collectivist morality was a powerful means of social control in the hands of the party.

This framework represents only the vertical concepts necessary in ordering the formal elements of the neo-Stalinist totalitarian-bureaucratic model. To complete the cognitive structure of this model, we have to explore the horizontal concepts, which delineate the operational factors in terms of goals-means relationships encompassing the promulgation of the Marxist shibboleth, known as the unity of theory and practice; the perversion of democratic principles; and the control of human behavior and development—all defined with reference to or in dependence on Marxist-Leninist philosophy. Apparently, the majority of mainline Sovietologists neglected to a considerable degree the fact that philosophical foundations (Aristotle would have called them "ruling principles") determine in the long run not only the direction and self-esteem of a society but also the conditions of its rise and fall.

Notes

1. G. K. Shakhnazarov, A. D. Boborykin, et al., *Social Science* (Moscow: Progress Publishers, 1977), 447.
2. Z., "To the Stalin Mausoleum," *Daedalus* 119, no. 1 (Winter 1990): 295–344.
3. Ibid., 298-99. Henceforth referred to as Z.
4. *Literaturnaia Gazeta* (Sept. 4, 1991): 9.
5. Iurii Afanas'ev, "Perestroika and Historical Knowledge," *Michigan Quarterly Review* (Fall 1989): 533–34.
6. "Sources," *Novyi Mir* no. 5 (1988).
7. Cited in *New York Review of Books* (December 19, 1991): 72.
8. Igor Klyamkin, "Why Is It Difficult to Tell the Truth?" *Novyi Mir* no. 2 (1989): 205.
9. *New York Review of Books* (December 19, 1991): 73.
10. 10. See Stephen Kotkin, "The Soviet Rustbelt," *The Harriman Institute Forum* 4, no. 2 (February, 1991): 1-16.
11. Alfred Evans, Jr., "The Decline of Soviet Socialism?" *Soviet Studies* (January, 1986): 11.
12. Alexander Dallin and Thomas B. Larsen, eds., *Soviet Politics Since Khrushchev* (Englewood Cliffs, N.J.: Prentice Hall, 1968), 57.
13. Ibid., 57–58.
14. Gordon B. Smith, *Soviet Politics—Continuity and Contradiction* (New York: St. Martin's Press, 1988), 209.
15. For a few excellent examples see Hans J. Morgenthau, *Politics among Nations*, 5th ed. (New York: Alfred A. Knopf, 1978); Karl W. Deutsch, *The Analysis of International Relations*, 2d ed. (Englewood Cliffs, N.J.: Prentice-Hall, 1978); and Stanley Hoffman, *The State of War: Essays in the Theory and Practice of International Relations* (New York: Praeger, 1965).
16. See, for example, Frederic J. Fleron, Jr., ed., *Communist Studies and the Social Sciences* (Chicago: Rand McNally, 1969), henceforth referred to as *Communist Studies*; Susan Gross Solomon, *Pluralism in the Soviet Union*

(New York: St. Martin's Press, 1983), henceforth referred to as *Pluralism*; and Erik P. Hoffman and Robin F. Laird, eds., *The Soviet Polity in the Modern Era* (Chicago: Aldine Publishing Co., 1984). For the thesis of "stability" as the great common characteristic of the Soviet Union and the United States, see Samuel P. Huntington, *Political Order in Changing Societies* (New Haven, Conn.: Yale University Press, 1968).

17. Z., 297–98.

18. Walter Z. Laqueur and Leopold Labedz, eds., *The State of Soviet Studies* (Cambridge, Mass.: MIT Press, 1965), 115.

19. Alexander J. Motyl, "Reassessing the Soviet Crisis," *Political Science Quarterly* 104, no. 2 (Summer 1989): 272–73.

20. Alexander J. Motyl, *Sovietology, Rationality, Nationality* (New York: Columbia University Press, 1990), 1.

21. Z., 298.

22. Stephen F. Cohen, *Rethinking the Soviet Experience* (New York and Oxford: Oxford University Press, 1985), 6.

23. *Communist Studies,* op. cit.

24. *Communist Studies*, 391–92.

25. Cited in David M. Ricci, *The Tragedy of Political Science* (New Haven and London: Yale University Press, 1984), 196.

26. Gabriel Almond and James Coleman, *The Politics of Developing Areas* (Princeton, N.J.: Princeton University Press, 1960), 16.

27. Cited in Ronald H. Chilcote, *Theories of Comparative Politics* (Boulder, Colo., Westview Press, 1981), 286.

28. Cited in Chilcote, *Theories*, 353.

29. Peter Rutland, "Sovietology: Notes for a Post-Mortem," *National Interest* (Spring 1993): 116.

30. Roger E. Kanet, ed., *The Behavioral Revolution in Communist Studies* (New York: Free Press, 1971).

31. Ibid., xi.

32. Vernon Van Dyke, *Political Science: A Philosophical Analysis* (Stanford, Calif.: Stanford University Press, 1960), 160.

33. Philip G. Roeder, *Soviet Political Dynamics* (New York: Harper & Row, 1988), 437-38.

34. Cited in Richard Pipes, "Gorbachev's Russia—Breakdown or Crackdown?" *Commentary* (March 1990): 13–25.

35. Solomon, *Pluralism*, 23. See also Milton Lodge, "Groupism in the Post-Stalin Period," *Midwestern Journal of Political Science* (August 1968): 330–51.

36. See Moshe Lewin, *The Gorbachev Phenomenon: A Historical Interpretation* (Berkeley, Calif.: University of California Press, 1991); and Frederick S. Starr, "Soviet Union: A Civil Society," *Foreign Policy* (Spring 1988): 26–41.

37. Vladimir Shlapentokh, *Soviet Intellectuals and Political Power—The Post-Stalinist Era* (Princeton, N.J.: Princeton University Press, 1990), 7.

38. Z., 301.

39. Smith, *Soviet Politics*, 102.

40. Theodore H. Friedgut, *Political Participation in the USSR* (Princeton, N.J.: Princeton University Press, 1979), 323, 325.
41. Ibid., 114–15.
42. Ibid., 88.
43. Zbigniew Brzezinski and Samuel P. Huntington, *Political Power—USA/USSR* (New York: Viking Press, 1964), 93.
44. Jerry Hough, *The Soviet Union and Social Science Theory* (Cambridge: Harvard University Press, 1977), 229.
45. Severyn Bialer, "The Political System," in *After Brezhnev: Sources of Soviet Conduct in 1980's,* ed. Robert F. Byrnes (Bloomington: Indiana University Press, 1983), 64–65. Emphasis added.
46. Cited in Nick Eberstadt, "The Latest Myths About the Soviet Union," *Commentary* (May 87): 21.
47. Z., 293.
48. Stanley Rothman and George W. Breslauer, *Soviet Politics and Society* (St. Paul, Minn.: West Publishing Company, 1978), 192.
49. Adam B. Ulam, *Stalin* (New York: The Viking Press, 1973).
50. Paul Cocks, Robert V. Daniels, and Nancy Whittier, eds., *The Dynamics of Soviet Politics* (Cambridge: Harvard University Press, 1976), 8.
51. Giovanni Sartori, "Concept Misinformation in Political Science," *American Political Science Review* (December, 1970): 1041.
52. Thomas S. Kuhn, *The Structure of Scientific Revolutions* (Chicago: University of Chicago Press, 1970), 93.
53. Cited in George W. Breslauer, *Five Images of the Soviet Union: Critical Review and Synthesis* (Berkeley, Calif.: University of California, Institute of International Studies, 1978), 23–24. Emphasis added.
54. George Orwell, "Politics and the English Language," in *Strategies in Prose*, ed. Wilfred A. Ferrell and Nicholas A. Salerno (New York: Holt, Rinehart & Winston, 1970), 323.
55. Benjamin R. Barber, "Conceptual Foundations of Totalitarianism," in *Totalitarianism in Perspective: Three Views*, ed. Carl J. Friedrich, Michael Curtis, and Benjamin R. Barber (New York: Praeger, 1969), 39.
56. Michael Walzer, *Radical Principles* (New York: Basic Books, 1980), 196.
57. Kotkin, "The Soviet Rustbelt," 5.
58. Leszek Kolakowski, "Amidst Moving Ruins," *Daedalus* (Spring 1992): 47. Emphasis added.
59. Cited in *Soviet Studies* 17, no. 4 (April, 1966): 475.
60. Jules Monnerot, *The Sociology of Communism* (Westport, Conn.: Greenwood Press, 1976), 257–58.
61. L. Kolakowski, "Totalitarianism and the Virtue of the Lie," in *Totalitarianism in Our Century*, ed. J. Howe (New York: Harper and Row, 1984), 123.
62. Z., 300–301.
63. Richard W. Wilson, "Political Pathology and Moral Orientations," *Comparative Political Studies* 24, no. 2 (July, 1991): 212.

64. Carl J. Friedrich and Zbigniew K. Brzezinski, *Totalitarian Dictatorship and Autocracy*, 2d ed. (Cambridge: Harvard University Press, 1965), 21.

65. Alex Inkeles, *Social Change in Soviet Russia* (Cambridge: Harvard University Press, 1968), 65–85. John S. Reshetar added four more "traits" to the model in *The Soviet Polity* (New York: Harper & Row, 1978).

66. The absence of the entry "totalitarianism" in the index of countless books on the Soviet Union is a striking example of the indifference and confusion in the field.

67. The rest of this chapter appeared in a slightly different form in Sigmund Krancberg, "1984: The Totalitarian Model Revisited," *Studies in Soviet Thought* 29 (1985): 71–77, © 1985 D. Reidel Publishing Company; it is reprinted here by permission of Kluwer Academic Publishers.

68. Neumann did not coin the term itself, which came into use in the late twenties.

69. George Orwell, *1984* (New York: Harcourt, Brace, Jovanovich, 1949), 185.

70. Carl J. Friedrich and Zbigniew K. Brzezinski, *Totalitarian Dictatorship and Autocracy* (Cambridge: Harvard University Press, 1956).

71. Carl J. Friedrich and Zbigniew K. Brzezinski, *Totalitarian Dictatorship and Autocracy*, 2d ed. (Cambridge: Harvard University Press, 1965).

72. Ibid., vii.

73. Ibid., 21.

74. Ibid., 22.

75. Ibid., 96–97.

76. The 26th Congress of the Communist Party of the Soviet Union, *Documents and Resolutions* (Moscow, 1981), 101.

77. *Marksistkaia Etika* (Moscow, 1976), 187–97.

78. The most interesting consideration of the "spirit" of collectivism is depicted in Aleksandr Zinov'ev, *The Yawning Heights* (New York: Random House, 1979).

79. John S. Reshetar, Jr., *The Soviet Polity* (New York: Dodd, Mead & Co. 1971); Samuel Huntington and Clement M. Moore, eds., *Authoritarian Politics in Modern Society* (New York: Basic Books, 1970); David Lane, *The Socialist Industrial State* (Boston: George Allen & Unwin, 1978). There is one inconsequential paragraph in Friedrich and Brzezinski's *Totalitarian Dictatorship and Autocracy*, 67.

80. Alfred G. Meyer, "The Soviet Political System," in *The USSR after 50 Years*, ed. Samuel Hendel and Randolph L. Braham (New York: Alfred Knopf, 1967), 52.

81. Gorbachev's difficulties and ultimate failure in confronting the inertia of Communist Party bureaucracy provide an illustration of the enduring force of Soviet bureaucratism.

82. Alfred G. Meyer, "Theories of Convergence," in *Change in Communist Systems*, ed. Chalmers Johnson (Stanford, Calif.: Stanford University Press, 1970), 325–26.

83. Friedrich and Brzezinski, *Totalitarian Dictatorship*, 2d ed., 218.

84. Ibid., 207.

85. Leszek Kolakowski, *Main Currents of Marxism* (Oxford: Clarendon Press, 1978), vol. III, 90.

86. Vaclav Havel, "Power of the Powerless," in *Living in Truth* (London: Faber & Faber, 1989), 43.

87. Some former Communists who are now posing as "democrats" are still passionately opposed to the process of privatization and to the ownership of farming land.

88. Merle Fainsod, *How Russia Is Ruled* (Cambridge: Harvard University Press, 1963), 421. Emphasis added.

89. Dissidents, such as Andrei Sinyavsky, Yuli Daniel, Iosif Brodsky, Andrei Amalrik, Valery Chalidze, Vladimir Bukovsky, Pavel Litvinov, Andrei Sakharov, and Alexander Solzhenitsyn—just to name a few—committed to freedom of thought and conscience amidst a political wasteland, were subjected to all forms of harsh and vindictive repressions, including exile.

Part Two

A Reappraisal of the Totalitarian Model: The Horizontal Concepts

2

The Unity of Theory and Practice in Historical Perspective

> The question whether objective truth can be attributed to human thinking is not a question of theory, but it is a *practical* question. In practice man must prove the truth, that is, the reality and power . . . of his thinking.
>
> Karl Marx, *Theses on Feuerbach*

In his brief graveside talk at the Highgate Cemetery on March 17, 1883, Engels, underscoring the revolutionary accomplishment of his lifelong friend, eulogized Marx as a theorist and thinker in the following passage:

> However great the joy with which we welcomed a new discovery in some theoretical science whose practical application perhaps it was as yet quite impossible to envisage, he experienced quite another kind of joy when the discovery involved immediate revolutionary changes in industry and in historical development in general.[1]

As if to demonstrate Marx's theoretical superiority, Engels published five years later the famous *Theses on Feuerbach*, discovered in an old volume by Marx—a finding that Engels appraised as the germ of a new worldview, invested with philosophical truths focused solely on "concurrence of changing circumstances and human activity . . . conceived and rationally understood only as *revolutionary practice*."[2]

Written in the spring of 1845 as a critique of Feuerbach's *Essence of Christianity*[3] and outlined in preparation for the more elaborate *German Ideology*, the eleven theses reflect Marx's attempt to remain within the traditional materialist framework concerning the general nature of knowledge, while trying to avoid the perplexities of answering time-honored questions addressed to the practical problems of man. Thus Marx set himself the task of developing a new form of materialism, supposedly free of the cobwebs of metaphysics, elucidating its

33

central principles in a fusion of theory and practice approached from the point of view of a human society or socialized humanity.

In pursuing this ambitious enterprise, Marx sharply challenged prevailing views of man's cognitive thought, which he considered to be based on a contemplative theory of knowledge, and which he attempted to unfold in the only paragraph comprising the first thesis.

Repudiating the idealistic trends of theoretical materialism—a materialism which lacks the insight into reality as it is experienced in all its intensity through sensation—Marx stated: "The chief defect of all hitherto existing materialism—that of Feuerbach included—is that the thing (*Gegenstand*), reality, sensuousness, is conceived only in the form of the object (*Object*) or of *contemplation* (*Anschauung*)."[4] In other words, Marx declared that the shortcomings of the existing materialism are apparent in the static world of conventional passivity, limiting the relation between man and the natural environment to a blend of sensory impressions and a reflective form of cognition. Incapable of divesting itself of the impediments of pure reason and abstract intellectual thinking, this kind of materialism lacks the vital elements of practical activity—that is, human activity which is purported to bring about a transformation of the natural environment in the pursuit of real, true knowledge.

However, Marx did not confine himself to the criticism of old-fashioned materialism, with its view of mechanical motion as the only form of motion. Marx's vision of the world embraced the more important aspects of motion as derived from the observation that the quintessence of man's life-existence is practical activity—a realm in which man is active in learning, in abstracting ideas from reality, and in forming ideas while interacting with reality. To be sure, the impulse to acquire knowledge for its own sake is of great value, simply because the desire to learn involves activity of the mind and enhances self-esteem. But according to Marx, accumulating knowledge is more than a passive absorption of ideas; it is an active and interdependent process that links the human mind with the external world and is manifested in "sensuous human activity" and "practice" (praxis).[5]

Despite the fact that the category of praxis arrived at in the first thesis is of special importance and is one of the seminal ideas in a world in which man gains his knowledge and experience through intersubjective activity, Marx neither explained nor defined praxis in the *Theses on Feuerbach*. Only in *The German Ideology*, written a year after the *Theses on Feuerbach*—a voluminous work that largely represents his fierce polemic with obscure and now forgotten Young Hegelians but devotes about sixty pages to a preliminary philosophical substantiation of historical materialism—do we find a double meaning for the notion of praxis. Even these descriptions of praxis are characterized by a certain level of abstraction that falls short of a rigorous, systematic clarification. This clarification would have to wait until 1859, when Marx wrote the *Critique of Political Economy*.[6]

In the first description of praxis in *The German Ideology*, Marx offered the following interpretation encompassing a number of properties unique to humankind:

> Where speculation ends—in real life—there real, positive science begins: the representation of practical activity (Praxis), of the practical process of development of man. . . . The production of ideas, of conceptions, of consciousness, is at first directly interwoven with the material activity and the material intercourse of man, the language of real life. . . . The same applies to mental production as expressed in the language of politics, laws, morality, religion and the metaphysics of a people.[7]

The second meaning of praxis is narrower in scope, incorporating the general orientation of Marxist thought, focused on the unitary process in human history—that is, on production in the economic sense of the term—manifested in the active role of the perceiving subject. This production process Marx extended on a social scale, to the productive activity of human beings:

> Man can be distinguished from animals by consciousness, by religion or anything else you like. They themselves begin to distinguish themselves from animals as soon as they begin to *produce* their means of subsistence, a step which is conditioned by their physical organization. By producing their means of subsistence men are indirectly producing their material life.[8]

These statements concerning the nature of praxis illuminate in general terms the major structural basis of Marxism, designating practical activity—e.g., tools, manufacturing, agriculture—as the generic core of productive labor and introduce in this fashion the foundations of historical materialism—the social philosophy of dialectical materialism. Making man's practical activity the decisive factor in the historical development of people in their production relations, Marx attempted to clarify his ideas in *The German Ideology*: "Our conceptions of history depend on our ability to expound the real process of production, starting out from the simple material production of life, and to comprehend the form of intercourse connected with this (i.e., civil society in its various stages), as the basis of all history."[9]

Reaffirming this kind of causal relation between the productive endeavors of humans and their epistemological achievements against the historical background, Marx stressed the self-externalization of the creative subject who finds his fulfillment in the most concise and famous formula of the "new" materialism: "It is not consciousness of men that determines their being, but, on the contrary, their social being determines their consciousness."[10]

This new conception of knowledge is closely related to objective reality, that is, a reality apprehended only if it is acted upon and shaped by humans and is best illustrated in a passage from C. E. M. Joad's *Guide to Philosophy*:

> The human being is like a coiled spring waiting to uncoil itself in action at the first touch of a stimulus from without. As the starting point of its action, it knows or is aware of the stimulus; but this knowledge, like the release of the spring, is only incidental. The true purpose of the human being's activity is not to know the stimulus but to change it. . . . Knowing is not an end in itself; we know in order to act. Knowledge cannot be understood, nor does it occur independently of its relation to action, the object of which is to change what is known.[11]

Thus, it is evident that the first thesis is devoted to human beings, how they think and act, shaping both themselves and their world in their quest for knowledge—a knowledge never detached from the environment of social reality. In addition, Marx suggested that praxis is not only of primary importance, it is also the foundation of all possible knowledge acquired within the framework of humankind's mode of activity. Moreover, praxis leads to the discovery of ever-increasing connections and relations in humankind's efforts at transforming reality—in other words, praxis leads to theory, to theoretical activity, representing an inseparable aspect of people's practical activity.

It should be remembered, however, that the first thesis and the two interpretations of praxis in *The German Ideology* were directed against Feuerbach's passive, contemplative materialism. Accordingly, Marx stated that the author of *The Essence of Christianity*, while glorifying the notion of a perfect religion, also overlooked the active aspects of human nature. Feuerbach dealt on one level with matter in the context of theory while, on the other level, he spoke in terms of mere feeling when he used the expression "man" instead of real historical man,[12] conceived in his given social connections. Equally, Feuerbach failed to grasp the true essence of praxis—in particular, the constructive nature of human consciousness in the realm of external objects, created as a result of practical, sensuous human activity. Hence, Marx concluded, Feuerbach's perception of "practice is conceived and determined only in its *dirty-judaic* practice form of appearance."[13]

In an attempt to emphasize that Feuerbach's view belongs to a supposedly lower stratum of human development—to the level of egoistic/utilitarian action—a number of Marxists and Crypto-Marxists "deodorized" this unfortunate passage with its unsavory adjective, substituting in its place Feuerbach's perception of praxis as "conceived and fixed only in its disgusting form."[14] Such an interpretation seems hardly related to man's efforts to transform reality in order to satisfy their concrete needs. Precisely because Feuerbach was unable to overcome the idealistic and superficial approach to the productive activities of man, Marx, rounding off the first thesis, concluded that Feuerbach did not "apprehend the significance of . . . 'revolutionary,' practical-critical activity,"[15] with all its ramifications.

What did the young Marx mean by "revolutionary," practical-critical activity? A careful reading of the first thesis does not furnish the answer, but a more explicit mention of revolutionary action is provided in the third thesis. A letter written by Marx in September 1843 includes some statements that might help clarify the phrase "revolutionary, practical-critical activity." In this letter to Arnold Ruge, Marx examined the theoretical tradition of Western philosophy, declaring that

> we have to concern ourselves with . . . the theoretical existence of man, that is religion, science, etc., and make it the object of our criticism, meaning in essence *the ruthless criticism of all that exists*, ruthless also in the sense that criticism does not fear its results and even less so a struggle with the existing powers.[16]

In his call for a ruthless criticism of all that exists, Marx left behind the dimension of philosophical speculation, turning instead to more practical goals set against the socio-political existence of man. Realizing that not everything is as it ought to be and dissatisfied with the status quo, man subjects this mode of existence to a sharp scrutiny, impervious to the reaction of the ruling authorities. According to Marx, man's practical-critical activity is distinguished by its "revolutionary" nature—a nature manifested in man's rebellious spirit and best expressed in a "criticism of and participation in politics, that is, in *real* conflicts, and identifying with them."[17]

It is noteworthy that, some decades later, Lenin, an avid student of Marx, also looked upon politics as a stagesetting of conflicts that leave no room for compromise or accommodation, and paraphrasing Karl von Clausewitz, Lenin approached the business of politics as the continuation of war by other means.

Part Two, Chapter Two

In the first thesis, Marx dispensed with cognitive thought as it is perceived from the perspective of the passive observer. Reaching out for a more adequate epistemological framework, Marx introduced a different determining factor instrumental to the acquisition of knowledge, namely, the driving force of the mind interacting on a practical level (praxis) with the subject. This approach to the act of knowing—that is, the immediate experience of the material world—enters into the very foundation of knowledge, transforming the attributes of knowing into a network of objective and subjective relations based on communal activities and interactions that are indissolubly tied to the unifying principle of man's productivity. According to Marx, "this mode of production . . . is a definite form of activity of individuals, a definite form of expressing their life, a definite *mode of life* on their part."[18]

Whether the young Marx, steeped in esoteric Hegelianism, was aware of having been anticipated by Sir Francis Bacon (1561–1626) is not known. It was Bacon who believed that humans should judiciously amass and interpret data, while conducting experiments to assert their mastery over the natural world. The inner workings of the processes by which knowledge should lead to immediate practical results are best described in Bacon's cognitive method—a method that will guarantee progress "from the close and strict union of the experimental and rational faculties."[19] Moreover, in *Novum Organum*, Bacon warned that

> neither the naked hand nor the understanding left to itself can effect much. It is by instruments and helps that the work is done, which are as much wanted for the understanding as for the hand. And as the instruments of the hand . . . give motion to guide it, so the instruments of the mind supply better suggestions for the understanding or cautions.[20]

Significantly, neither Bacon nor Marx was unable to overcome the epistemological dichotomy inherent in the perception of the material world when this world is transformed into a comprehensible idea, in which subject and object are interrelated and, so to speak, are involved in each other. Obviously, this relation between two realms—the material world and the human cognitive drive—turns the pursuit of knowledge into distinctions of fact and judgment or, if we put this elemental point in slightly different language, between mind and matter.

Accordingly, for Marx, man is not divided into one half that knows and another half that acts. And indeed, in *The German Ideology*, Marx attempts—with mixed success—to free himself from this sense of ambiguity as he elevates practical activity (praxis) to the level of productive labor manifested in the socio-economic development of man. If Hegel tried to maintain an integrative unity between thought and being, so did the young Marx assume a high degree of coincidence between man and reality, which in its coextensive relationship and mutually causal interaction must lead to "the production of ideas, of conceptions, of consciousness . . . directly interwoven with the material activity and the material intercourse of man."[21] For Marx, this continuous process of transition and interaction between man and reality, characterized by a genuinely indivisible synthetic unity, represents the real language of life—a language that is no longer satisfied with mere reflection, passive contemplation or reconstructive analysis.

Thus, with the role of activity explored in the practical process of human development, real knowledge has to take its place while humans are imposing their forms on the external world, creating and transforming the environment through a conscious, productive effort. On this point, then, Marx—somewhat different in tone from Bacon—defines man as a cognitive being in possession of epistemological certainty, attained thanks to the practical aspect of knowledge, and ascribes to the human mind a grasp of reality *only* if reality is acted upon.

However, this certainty of knowledge achieved in a practically conditioned world is a problematic phase in the human perception of reality. This certainty, even if closely related to human sensuous-practical activity, encounters a new critical relation when the problem of truth, with its own norms and criteria, enters the scene.

Philosophers who turn a critical eye on specific areas of human endeavor try to avoid making assumptions that are vague, obscure or unfounded. Their chief contribution is aptly characterized by Alfred North Whitehead, one of the more prominent and respected thinkers of modern times, who perceived the virtues of philosophy as "insight and foresight, and a sense of the worth of life, in short, that sense of importance which nerves all civilized effort."[22] It is because of this coordinating spirit of philosophy—a spirit which "nerves all civilized effort"—that some thinkers are inclined to believe in an orderly world where the uncertain and the changeable are distinguished from the relatively permanent, while the accidental and the unique are differentiated and screened from the universally valid. Many different examples of this generalized world view are suitably represented in the traditional philosophic discussion of truth—a discussion distinguished by a rich if checkered past, dominated through the ages by the correspondence theory and the coherence theory of truth.[23]

The correspondence theory, which has its roots in antiquity, maintains that truth consists in the satisfaction of a relationship between what we would normally call an assertion or proposition and a fact (or state of affairs) in the real world. Adherents of this "common sense" theory maintain that the term "correspondence" points more precisely to a relationship in which propositions mesh with reality in a satisfactory way. As is well known, the correspondence theory is open to a number of objections, one of which is particularly damaging: in claiming that truth is independent of us and our language, the proponents of the correspondence theory fail to analyze in a convincing manner the relation of correspondence—a term that philosophers deem to be indefinable—to nonlinguistic phenomena. In other words, a linguistic sign may be related to but does not necessarily "correspond" to the objects it signifies. Furthermore, to make things even more complicated, if the term "correspondence" implies a relationship, it is quite obvious that not every relationship is one of correspondence.

In contrast, the defenders of the coherence theory claim that truth does not consist of a relation (or correspondence) between judgment and fact (or a given state of affairs). Instead, they offer the coherence theory in which truth is established by the coherent relation of a statement with a system of other statements, all of which are taken to be true. Since the verification process in this theory stresses a genuineness of coherence rather than the descriptive accuracy of a matter of fact, the great difficulty arises in discovering whether the logical connection (or consistency) among ideas, judgments, and facts is true or false. Needless to say, each such "coherent" statement demands a careful and exhaustive investigation before anything may be accepted as true or false.

The two traditional theories clearly unfold the contradictory tendencies in humanity's effort to obtain valid, verifiable knowledge in the search for truth. Moreover, both theories share a common weakness that is not always acknowledged by the opposing philosophical schools. A careful analysis of the correspondence and coherence theories shows that the two theories—in the process of logical discourse, designed to move away from error and toward truth—are actually reduced to the art of working with concepts structured in beliefs (or disbeliefs). And it is this movement that is articulated in linguistic accounts of matter of fact, subject to shades and degrees of meaning that expose the limitations of our language regarding the possibility of correct expression and interpretation. Thus the breakdown of our metaphoric language into things and attributes, or substances and qualities, that emerge in spatial determinations against the backdrop of temporal relations presents a whole, intricate complex of crucial issues, which forms the subject matter of endless disputes between rival philosophical theories.

Apparently, the young Marx was well aware of the obstacles to achieving a practical and effective dimension of truth by using the conceptual schemes of the two traditional theories. Furthermore, Marx was undoubtedly cognizant of the fact that Hegel, who is distinguished by his complete rejection of the agnostic standpoint in epistemology, assumed that the universe is penetrable to human thought and, consequently, that there is a reality outside the mind which the mind can know. Thus Hegel states in his *Logic* that "truth may be ascertained by several methods, with experience . . . as the first of these methods, for in experience everything depends upon the mind we bring to bear upon actuality. A great mind is great in its experience."[24]

Heavily indebted to Hegel, Marx goes one step further in the operational definition of truth, and challenging the presuppositions of the traditional theories, he finds that the stress on observation and passive contemplation is fundamentally wrong and declares that the question of truth can never be settled by abstract argumentation. Amplifying this criticism of traditional theories of truth, Marx states in the second thesis on Feuerbach, that "objective truth (*gegenständliche Warheit*) is not a question of theory, but a *practical* question."[25] This question is framed in terms of a cognitive function, accentuating the role of the subject in the very realization of truth within reality. Consequently, for Marx, truth is not only essential in molding reality but is—first and foremost—a practical function, performed with a view to satisfying human needs and drives, including the most mundane aspects of existence such as food and shelter. This is Marx's picture of the cognitive process—*a process of continuous advancement toward a full knowledge of objective reality, with practical activity (praxis) deciding the extent of its truth.*

Thus praxis is declared as the criterion for evaluating truth claims based on evidence that is verified by its capability of testing incontrovertible matters of fact. How does praxis test these truths? How do we define objectively a valid verification procedure? For Marx, the answer is obvious: "In practice, man is bound to prove the truth, that is, the reality and force, the thisworldliness of his thinking."[26] Again, Marx is stressing the importance of human effort, the efficacy of human will in action when testing beliefs on the basis of their expected consequences—by their reality and force. Hence, the *true* will work; but Marx did not tell us that it does not necessarily follow that whatever works is *true*.

It is noteworthy that Francis Bacon, who also trusted the practical sense of humankind more than its intellectual faculties, devotes his attention to the reality and force of man's power over nature, to be obtained by a complete knowledge of its secrets. As Bacon states: "Where human knowledge and human power meet in one . . . all that man can do is to put together or put asunder natural bodies. The rest is done by nature working within."[27]

A somewhat similar but more developed idea, expressed with more confidence afforded by practice, appears in *Capital* when Marx theorizes on the practical aspects of human labor process: "Labor is, in the first place, a process in which both man and Nature participate, and in which man of his own accord starts, regulates, and controls the material reactions between man and Nature."[28]

It is now evident that there are many truths in the world of Karl Marx, and these various truths are no longer static in their specific nature, because they are constantly changing in a developmental progression that Marx called "dialectical"—a process in which

> the material phenomenon alone can serve as its starting point. Such an inquiry will confine itself to the confrontation and comparison of a fact, not with ideas, but with another fact. For this inquiry, the one thing of moment is, that both facts be investigated as accurately as possible, and that they actually form, each with respect to the other, different moments of an evolution; but most important of all is the rigid analysis of the series of successions, of the sequences and concatenations in which the different stages such as evolution present themselves.[29]

Assessing the consequences of this view for an understanding of "knowledge" and "truth," one cannot escape the conclusion that Marx failed to address himself in the *Theses on Feuerbach* to the conduct and analysis of inquiry. Such inquiry should involve making choices, collecting material data, and testing hypotheses to allay any doubts in forming practical judgments regarding the means and ends of this scholarly enterprise.

Setting out to survey the principal concerns of epistemology, some philosophers reach the conclusion that the relation between knowledge and truth in the *Theses on Feuerbach* is formulated in a manner corresponding to the philosophical thought of John Dewey known as pragmatism or instrumentalism. In fact, early American Marxists, despite their political disagreements with the representatives of pragmatism, assumed a friendly neutrality in their efforts to reconcile and mold together the two philosophical tendencies.[30] However, it seems that these efforts to bring Marx and Dewey into a substantial agreement in their treatment of knowledge and truth derive from the superficial resemblance between the practical foundations of instrumentalism and the text of the first two theses on Feuerbach. To be sure, on first impression and in both instances, the discovery of truth becomes a practical and problematic activity anchored in socio-historical circumstances. Still, to anyone who has learned to see with critical eyes the approach to epistemology in the *Theses on Feuerbach* and the exploration of cognitive categories leading to the scientific method in John Dewey's *Logic: The Theory of Inquiry*,[31] it is most evident that the different style and focus of analysis by each author leads to dissimilar intentions, judgments, and goals.

Attributing to education a major role in developing a genuine democratic community, and labeling his philosophy as experimentalism or instrumentalism, Dewey regarded ideas as being essentially instruments for the solution of problems in our socio-political and cultural environment. For Dewey, "the criterion of the worth of an idea is the capacity of the idea to operate in fulfilling the object for the sake of which it was projected. Capacity of operation in this fashion is the test, measure, or the criterion of truth."[32]

Thus Dewey's concept of knowledge—even considered from the vantage point of the reflexive act of knowing—is empirical, practical as well as operational, permitting us to test more effectively the validity and usefulness of knowledge claims posited in the course of a scholarly inquiry. But this definition is far from sufficient to grasp what Dewey really intended. On a purely philosophical plane, Dewey attempted to refine the method of pragmatism into a coherent framework that was designed to integrate valid knowledge with the practical coordinates of human competence. The complexity and magnitude of this enterprise gives rise to the intellectual process of inquiry—the dynamic center of Dewey's philosophy. For Dewey, in addressing a large range of problems, inquiry performs a decisive function in the assessment of human potentialities as weighed against the anticipation of consequences. Thus inquiry can best be defined as the "directed transformation of an indeterminate situation into which one that is so determinate in its constituent distinctions and relations as to convert the elements of the original situation into a unified whole."[33]

This kind of logical and practical merger of thought and action leads to the progressive development of Dewey's ideal of knowledge, encompassed in the ultimate triumph of a practical-minded rationality. This ideal is expressed in the definition of a scientific pragmatism based on Peirce's view of truth, which Dewey cites approvingly in his *Logic*: "Truth is the concordance of an abstract statement which the ideal limit towards which endless investigation would tend to bring scientific belief."[34]

It is therefore surprising that Bertrand Russell, in his analysis of the *Theses of Feuerbach*, concludes that "allowing for a certain difference in phraseology, this (Marxist) doctrine is essentially indistinguishable from instrumentalism."[35] In the same manner, and without questioning the presuppositions and the forms of Marxist thought or principles, Corliss Lamont fundamentally agrees with Russell's conclusion when he states, "It is incontestable in my opinion that the main import and intent of Dewey's massive philosophical system is thoroughly anti-idealistic and in agreement with the general world-view of dialectic materialism."[36]

Even more remarkable is the fact that, in the same time frame (ca. 1940), the young Sidney Hook—still under the spell of Karl Marx and deeply involved in left-wing politics—attempted to transform Marxism in its nineteenth-century content into a twentieth-century philosophy by bringing it close to a substantial identity with Dewey's instrumentalism. According to Hook, "Marxism . . . appears in the main as a huge judgment of practice, in Dewey's sense of the phrase, and its truth or falsity (instrumental adequacy) is an experimental matter. Believing it and acting upon it helps to make it true or false."[37]

Carried away by one of the instrumentalist principles that was based on the premise that truth is nothing but the successful working of an idea, Hook embellished further his transformation scheme, proclaiming the Father of Communism as a precursor of Dewey, while arguing that in matters concerning the relation to material reality, language, and thought, the great American philosopher is the "most outstanding and legitimate heir of Marxism."[38]

Now, in retrospect, it is quite clear that Bertrand Russell's attempt to link together Marx and Dewey was the result of a presumptuous and somewhat careless reading of the *Theses on Feuerbach*. Only a few years after the publication of his essay "Dewey's New Logic," Russell retracted his statement, declaring that Dewey "has never been a Marxist"[39] and that dialectical materialism, with its dogmatic Communist philosophy, resembles a traditionally orthodox theology, attempting to present a theoretical expression of a particular religion.

By comparison, the effort of Corliss Lamont and Sidney Hook to join together the logical system of a "bourgeois" philosophy with the preestablished dissonance of a materialist dialectic conveys the impression of an undertaking designed to dilute the essential tenets of Marxist ideology, in order to overcome the social and philosophical isolation of Marxism from the mainstream of American politics in the thirties and forties. It is also obvious that Hook and Lamont attempted to secure a greater acceptance and academic respectability for the principles of dialectical materialism with the intellectual community.

A careful analysis of the *Theses on Feuerbach* shows that the firm resolve to bring Marx and Dewey into substantial identity is argued from false and deceptive premises that are based on a faulty analogy. The irony is that Marxists pride themselves on being realistic, but Sidney Hook and Corliss Lamont, in their appraisal of instrumentalism and its supposedly close relation to dialectical materialism, failed to take into account that Dewey was never attracted to a study of Marxism and that with his marked respect for the scientific method, Dewey could hardly have found any merits in the ideological neo-obscurantism, masquerading under the guise of "dialectical enlightenment," to be gained through dialectical reasoning.[40] Moreover, truly interested in what unites men and not in what divides them, Dewey had little regard for the Marxist concept of class struggle. Placing himself within the intellectual tradition of Western culture, John Dewey, unlike Marx, held that "both 'laissez faire' and 'socialistic' doctrines are obfuscations . . . preventing us from analyzing our problems freely and asking ourselves which of these principles might be more likely to resolve the particular problem with which we are faced."[41]

This political view—so significant in its sharp contrast with Marx's social scientific pretensions built on revolutionary expectations—is even more conspicuous when we take into consideration the instrumentalist concept of knowledge in terms of its function and usefulness. For Dewey, the figurative description of the basic relation between knowledge and its function is embodied in the strict sense of natural science, that is, a scientific knowledge of a type that has given up all dependency on ideological preconceptions in their many forms. Given this fact, all scientific concept formation begins with the "necessity of experiment for determination of data and for the use of ideas and conceptions—including principles and laws—as directive hypotheses,"[42] which are used as a guiding norm in the transition from one established and verified link to another and which may be defined as the building blocks of scientific knowledge. Thus, from the heights of its theoretical and practical ideals, the scientific outlook becomes Dewey's foremost principle in the pursuit of relevant knowledge—a knowledge that touches every major area of political and cultural life and is predicated on the improvement of social conditions coextensive with the development of thought in science and philosophy.

In contrast to Dewey, Marx, who—with the exception of his many exercises in political pamphleteering—subjected himself in *Capital* to a rigorous scientific methodology, does not offer a theory of science; nor does he show any interest in the problem of the relationship between philosophy and science.[43] To be sure, Marx, who devoted his energies to a substantial critique of political economy, makes a few superficial remarks on the issue of the scientific method in the preface to the first edition of *Capital*. Likewise, in the introduction to his *Grundrisse*, Marx in general terms and in Hegelian fashion distinguishes two paths of scientific analysis: the passage from the concrete to the abstract and the passage from the abstract to the concrete. Marx adds that it seems to be correct to begin with the real and concrete, in the sense of what is actual.[44]

But what really separates Marx from Dewey is the fact that, in contrast to the great American philosopher, Marx belongs to the family of thinkers who are more aware of what divides men than of what unites them. Investing his materialistic conception of human history with dialectical qualities, Marx views society as a conglomerate of collectivities and individuals torn by schisms and rent with ceaseless universal conflict—a conflict that finds its expression in the concept of a class struggle, elevated in his political pamphlets to a militant program for violent revolutionary action. Convinced that he has mastered the laws of history, Marx proclaims in the *Communist Manifesto* that "the history of all hitherto existing society is the history of class struggles,"[45] overlooking the fact that a greater part of human history has been devoid of the kind of revolutionary change that tears apart the whole structure which holds authority and hierarchy together in the established order. And even if socio-historical relations are dialectical in character,[46] these relations not only engender social contradictions and conflict but also give birth to social interdependence and reciprocity, which contribute a certain sense of social equilibrium required for the survival of society. It is surprising that Marx—a historian in his own right—finds himself driven to explain the meaning of history in terms of class struggles without mentioning racial struggles, national struggles,[47] and religious struggles.[48]

However, just as Engels, in his parting words at Highgate Cemetery, characterized his friend as "before all else a revolutionist," Marx—true to his lifelong calling and preoccupation—assumed in the *Theses*

The Unity of Theory and Practice 47

on Feuerbach that even a theory of knowledge may be identified with a particular political point of view. If, for Dewey, the ideal of knowledge is to become natural science, Marx—warding off the hand of science in the third thesis on Feuerbach—trespasses beyond the scientific goal and, relapsing into the realm of violent political action, takes an approach to the world of knowledge qualitatively different from that argued about in traditional philosophy.

The effect of this sweeping reorientation is demonstrated in a few vague statements in the third thesis, which offer a new and apodictic basis for Marx's political thinking when he declares that "it is men who change circumstances" and, taking for granted the underlying historical necessity revealed in this mode of activity, Marx adds that the changing of circumstances "can be conceived and rationally understood only as *revolutionary* practice."[49] Viewed from the standpoint of Marxist epistemology, the violent overthrow of the existing order involves more than just the changing of circumstances; it also entails a revolutionary transformation of human consciousness and a radical realignment of cognitive categories as reflected in the process of drastic socio-political change, which, in its accelerated development, represents for Marx the real, actual world. Thus, in stressing the significance of free will and human effort in the revolutionary act of waging the class war, Marx, as a Hegelian, joined freedom and determinism in a dialectical unity, proclaiming dogmatically that truth is inherent only in a revolutionary practice conducive to an optimal success in the class struggle.

It is fair to say that the general movement of ideas in the first three theses on Feuerbach—marked by the epistemological "breakthrough" leading to the brief outline of a program that stands for Marx's usurpation of the unchallengeable right to advance a violent form of direct action, designed to overthrow the "old" order—is formulated in terse, shorthand expressions in which Marx fails to provide an explicit characterization of the descriptive and normative meanings of the textual arrangement. This does not mean that the entire text of the *Theses on Feuerbach* and Marx's active intervention in changing the course of history are open to philosophical imagination or haphazard interpretation. Any delusion of this kind is dispelled by the generally accepted view that the *Theses on Feuerbach* endure in their significance because they have to be considered as a compact prolegomena to *The German Ideology*. But this conclusion is only partly accurate. A study of the *Theses on Feuerbach* in conjunction with the *Communist Manifesto* and the *Address of the Central Committee to the Communist League* shows clearly a well-established correlation among the three works, with the *Theses on Feuerbach* serving as a primary note of reference to the other two memorable political pamphlets.

One of the most powerful political documents of our time, the *Communist Manifesto* presents in highly provocative and inflammatory language a call to the working classes to rise in revolt against the existing bourgeois order. Despite his mistaken belief that Germany will be the birthplace of the communist revolution, Marx—with some assistance from Engels—proclaims the revolutionary role of the proletariat everywhere, thus projecting the violent overthrow of all existing social conditions as a universal phenomenon.[50] Echoing the eleventh and most famous thesis on Feuerbach—"the philosophers have only *interpreted* the world, in various ways; the point, however, is to *change* it"[51]—Marx elucidates a detailed plan of action (the ten regulations) for the future proletarian government, specified in a number of steps aimed at a violent rearrangement of the existing property relations. That ideas have consequences is the insight of the instrumentalist, matter-of-fact view of the world. And yet, when we read the *Communist Manifesto*, with its passionate call to a general revolt, it becomes all the clearer that *ideas are weapons*—a principle that epitomizes the whole spirit of Marxism. Here again, we are facing the fusion of materialism with a doctrine of human will, which is manifested in the forcible expropriation of the capitalists, while Marx spells out "the first step in the revolution," calling for the elevation of the "proletariat to the position of ruling class."[52] Strangely enough, this declaration of unlimited war against the existing social order clarifies in general terms some constitutive factors of the proletariat in commanding positions but never explains the essential components of revolutionary practice.

Only two years after the publication of the *Manifesto* did Marx succeed in formulating a detailed grammar of action, proposing a number of precise observations concerning the meaning and sharp-edged scenario of revolutionary practice. Confident that a successful proletarian revolution was close at hand, Marx prepared with Engels, early in 1850, an *Address of the Central Committee to the Communist League*.[53]

In this *Address*, Marx assumed that the next revolutionary wave in Germany would carry the democratic petite bourgeoisie to power, with its main goal being "to consolidate their position in their own interests."[54] Marx branded as intolerable the kind of democracy promulgated by the petit bourgeois faction, calling for a popular government and social reforms "behind which their special interests are concealed."[55] To oppose the policies of the new petit bourgeois government, the revolutionary workers' party was to "establish an independent, secret and public organization . . . alongside the official democrats,"[56] independent of bourgeois influence. Moreover, the democrats were not to be allowed to consolidate their hold on power, with the armed proletariat dictating such conditions to the democrats that their rule would, from the outset, bear within it the seeds of their downfall. To destabilize further the democratic government, the restoration of law and order was to be opposed by encouraging "instances of popular revenge against hated individuals or public buildings" and by spreading "unconcealed mistrust in the new government"[57] that represented the petit bourgeois party.

Marx further declared that, after assisting the petit bourgeois party in winning the revolution, the workers "must establish simultaneously their own revolutionary workers' governments, whether in the form of municipal committees and municipal councils or in the form of workers' clubs or workers' committees."[58] (This is where, in 1917, Lenin learned to utilize the Soviets, or councils. The resemblance becomes even more unmistakable when the *Address* goes on to stress the need to centralize the workers' councils and provide them with proletarian, red guards.) The workers were not to be deceived by the "democratic talk of freedom for the communities, of self-government, etc."—the goal must be "the most determined centralization of power in the hands of the state authority,"[59] after the overthrow of the petit bourgeois government.

It is obvious from the text of the *Address* that the concept of democracy as a progressive socio-political program was of little value to Marx even before it had the opportunity to prove itself. As for the prescriptive nature of revolutionary practice in the *Address*, it is difficult to appraise its theoretical and empirical value, since it is a well-recognized fact that there have been no socialist revolutions in advanced capitalist countries. Still, an objective assessment of the program of action ultimately grounded in revolutionary practice shows that the *Address* is strangely silent about the human cost of the revolution, the great toll in human suffering, and the incalculable losses incurred as a result of the violent overthrow of existing social conditions.

Furthermore, an additional feature of the *Address* is usually ignored by Marxologists, namely, that Marx's theory and practice of revolution do not protect society against revolutionary terrorism. On the contrary, as the revolutionary who rejected his society's values, Marx accommodates the revolutionary will and candidly calls for acts of terror in carrying out "popular revenge against hated individuals."

Moreover, oblivious to the catastrophic loss of human life and the dreadful economic hardships of protracted, costly civil wars, Marx stated in 1850: "We must say to the workers—you will have to go through fifteen or twenty years of civil wars and international wars not only in order to change extant conditions, but also in order to change yourselves and to render yourselves fit for political dominion."[60] Almost one hundred and forty years later, as if in confirmation of Marx's dire prophecy, the Russian writer J. Bogomolov, commenting on the disturbing developments in the Soviet Union, declared that "civil war has acquired the character of a pattern in our day-to-day existence."[61]

Undoubtedly, Marx's attitude of indifference to the catastrophic costs of revolution and civil war was superseded by an apocalyptic vision of humanity's liberation from the age-old oppression only by means of the revolutionary enterprise. Thus Marx lived the dream of a future "perfect" communist society, never considering the probability of fundamental differences between the intended and actual socio-political effects of revolutionary action—a distinct likelihood with the intrusion of new and unexpected factors in revolutionary and post-revolutionary circumstances—a development that in the twentieth century did result in unforeseen and disastrous consequences.[62]

It is true that with the prospect of revolution receding into the distant future, Marx mellowed somewhat and recognized the importance of democratic reforms in improving the lot of the working class. Many years later, Marx and Engels admitted that the *Address* was written at a time of illusion and ill-founded hopes. Nonetheless, their extremist views as expressed in the *Address* were never explicitly repudiated, and their main objectives—the extinction of the bourgeoisie and the establishment of the dictatorship of the proletariat—remained unaffected.[63]

In a letter written in September of 1879, Engels, forever devoted to the theory and practice of revolution, declared that "for almost forty years we have stressed the class struggle as the immediate driving power of history and in particular the class struggle between bourgeoisie and proletariat as the great lever of the modern social revolution; it is therefore, impossible for us to cooperate with people who wish to expunge this class struggle."[64]

A number of social scientists consider Marx's early writings as "mere preliminaries or juvenilia, citing Engels's embarrassed remark made in the 1880s that they were as unimportant as Marx's youthful poetry and unreadable in their semi-Hegelian language."[65]

Still, taking comfort in Marx's juvenile fragments of philosophical idealism, interlaced with flashes of political liberalism, some social scientists offer the view that the early writings—also known as the *Economic and Philosophical Manuscripts of 1844*[66]—provide a key to the "true humanization of man" and to the "release of the richness of human nature."[67] Curiously enough, these students of Marxism also tend to ignore or minimize the significance of the *Theses on Feuerbach*, even going so far as to find virtue in the sheer length of the *Economic and Philosophical Manuscripts of 1844*, which comprise more than one hundred and seventy pages in the *Historisch-kritische Gesamtausgabe*[68] whereas, by comparison, the *Theses on Feuerbach* consist only of eleven sentences or semi-paragraphs.[69]

This attempt to belittle or ignore the celebrated *Theses on Feuerbach*—the first outline of Marx's revolutionary postulates that matured into a political party and a program—hardly qualifies as a valid analysis of Marx's political thought. Obviously, a sharp separation exists between the quantitative "given"—i.e., the volume and length of a work in the number of pages—and the guiding principles of scholarly exegesis firmly rooted in content, substance, and insight. No doubt it is this consideration that prompted major biographers of Marx to characterize the *Economic and Philosophical Manuscripts of 1844* as "a sketchy and derivative work containing more philosophy than economics"[70] and representing "no more than a starting point for Marx—an initial, exuberant outpouring of ideas to be taken up and developed in subsequent writings."[71]

A more serious error, however, is involved with the disregard on the part of some writers for well-established facts. Such writers, enamored of the philosophic humanism of the youthful Marx, attribute to him a rather peaceful vision of socialism before 1848, "defined in terms of human aspirations and potentialities"[72]—a turn of phrase more readily applied nowadays to the image of a "socialism with a human face." Be this as it may, it is evident that as early as 1844, Marx—not yet quite clear in his longings to save the world—published his *Critique of Hegel's Philosophy of Right: Introduction* in the ill-fated *Deutsch-Französische Jahrbücher*, proclaiming "praxis as the goal of true philosophy (i.e., as criticism of speculative philosophy) and revolution as the true praxis."[73] Only a year later, Marx, in the *Holy Family*—stressing the inevitability of a socialist revolution—stated that "it is the task of the proletariat, to which its historical situation obviously and irrevocably destined it, to take action to set historical development free, and to execute sentence upon capitalist private property which, by its creation of the proletariat, has brought sentence upon itself."[74]

In the analysis of human beings, events, and movements, the goals of social science depend on the type of explanatory methods formed in a system of conceptual claims that combine aggregates or configurations of actions, relations, and circumstances. This approach entails the logical interpretation of sociological and historical explanations, which are seldom reduced to the uncertainty of what is known as "psychological" terms. Perhaps this is one of the reasons why students of Marxism, bent on analyzing the categories of economic and social transformation, overlook the fact that Marx, from the very beginning of his intellectual life, was double-sided. On the one hand, Marx was drawn to a concept of praxis directed toward a critique of speculative philosophy—a critique coupled with the conviction that only through their practical endeavors would humans acquire knowledge of the external world, thereby raising knowledge to a level that places practice in the primary position in a changing reality. Thus, while reaffirming the opposition between theory and praxis, the young Marx, in 1844, attributed to praxis its superiority over theory, declaring that "the resolution of theoretical contradictions is possible only in a practical way, *only* through the practical energy of man."[75] And again, a year later, Marx propounded the same assertion, although somewhat differently phrased, in the second thesis on Feuerbach, without any attempt to substantiate his claim.

On the other hand, Marx was intensely attracted to the notion of a "revolutionary praxis," a praxis imbued with the concept of revolutionary change, perceived by Marx as the most basic component of the historical process in which "material power must be overthrown by material power."[76] Accordingly, the quintessence of "revolutionary praxis" manifested itself throughout Marx's intellectual and political life in a relentless, warlike posture against the "bourgeois" social order—an attitude distinguished by an entirely different criterion from the epistemological sense of praxis. This criterion, briefly discussed earlier, was based on Marx's understanding of history[77] as a forum for incessant class warfare, culminating in the victory of the proletariat. Obviously, the assumption underlying Marx's attitude toward praxis from the early writings to his more mature works demonstrates a double focal point on both epistemology and revolutionary politics, never raising the question of whether it is theoretically feasible to include two entirely different conceptual schemes under the heading of a single concept of praxis, much less providing a clear definition of the term "theory."

This twofold outlook on praxis, conceived and articulated by Marx, was readily accepted by Engels, for whom praxis was likewise a revolutionary goal, clearly presented in the need for the creation of a social revolution, leading to a new and better society—a goal that elevated violence to a tactical weapon of revolution.[78] That Engels, like Marx, was burdened with a sense of ambiguity on the subject of praxis is quite clearly exemplified in references related to the autonomy of the individual in his quest for valid knowledge within the boundaries of theory and practice. Thus, in the introduction to the English edition of *Socialism: Utopian and Scientific*, first published in 1880, Engels declared, "Before there was argument there was action. *Im Anfang war die Tat.* (In the beginning was the deed). . . . And human action had solved the difficulty long before human ingenuity invented it. The proof of the pudding is in the eating."[79]

Only a few years later, in 1886, Engels stated again in a more luminous manner:

> There is yet a set of different philosophers—those who question the possibility of any cognition, or at least of an exhaustive cognition of the world. . . . The most telling refutation of this (scepticism and agnosticism) as of all other philosophical crotchets, is praxis, namely experiment and industry.[80]

Engels attempts to make his point by arguing from the philosophical premises that his presuppositions are correct, because, corresponding to the tenets of dialectical materialism, the world is material and our knowledge is held to be derived from the world itself. Still, as if anticipating the question of testing and proving the relationship of theory to practice or to experiment and industry, Engels adds that:

> from the moment we turn these objects to our own use, according to the qualities we perceive in them, we put to an infallible test the correctness or otherwise of our sense perceptions. If these perceptions have been wrong, then our estimate of the use to which an object can be turned must also be wrong, and our attempt must fail. But if we succeed in accomplishing our aim, we find that the object does agree with our idea of it, and does answer the purpose we intended it for, then that is positive proof that our perceptions of it, and of its qualities, so far, agree with reality outside ourselves. . . . This line of reasoning seems undoubtedly hard to beat by mere argumentation.[81]

The realization that immediate knowledge acquired by our sense perception need not be proved by argument but by practice,[82] experiment, or industry inspired Engels with an optimism eagerly shared by the father of Russian Marxism, Georgi Plekhanov. It was Plekhanov who, in his early works, attempted to analyze the interaction of historical forces at the turn of the century, emphasizing the role and function of a Russian Marxist party in advancing the political and economic goals of the workers in building a radically new world. In his undertaking to convert the Russian revolutionary movement to Marxism, Plekhanov found the master key to reality in the reconciliation of theory and practice—the early forerunner of the later "unity of theory and practice"[83]—stating with confidence: "It is self-evident that every theoretical conclusion concerning the capacity of a given class or stratum for definite practical action always requires a certain degree of verification by experience, and that, consequently, it can be considered true *a priori* only within certain, more or less broad limits."[84]

Convinced that "Marx discovered the internal causes of the historical progress of mankind" and that "it remained only to examine Russian social relations from his point of view,"[85] Plekhanov expressed skepticism regarding the merits of revolutionary praxis, stressing the absolute necessity of a developed capitalism in Russia as a precondition to the introduction of socialism. "If socialism is imposed by force," he predicted in a warning that went unheeded, "it will inescapably lead to a political deformity after the image of the Chinese and Peruvian Empires, a renewed Czarist despotism with a Communist lining."[86]

Accusing Plekhanov of practicing "the noble sport of sophistry" and of shamelessly distorting the main thesis of dialectics,[87] Lenin revitalized the revolutionary aspect of praxis, placing class warfare at the center of the political struggle—a struggle to be led by a tightly organized and disciplined party, the workers' vanguard. Determined that this vanguard party, the Bolsheviks, must take power, Lenin penned in the waning months of 1917 an open call to rebellion, declaring that

> all hopes for a peaceful development of the Russian revolution have vanished for good. . . . Let us have no constitutional or republican illusions of any kind, no more illusions about a peaceful path. . . . Let us gather forces, reorganize them, and resolutely prepare for the armed uprising. . . . The aim of the insurrection can only be to transfer power to the proletariat, supported by the poor peasants, with a view to putting our Party programme into effect.[88]

Evaluating Lenin's dynamic emphasis on revolutionary praxis, account must also be taken of his ambivalent view of the epistemological aspect of praxis. Lenin proclaims Marx's teachings as a "consummate philosophical materialism which has provided mankind, and especially the working class, with powerful instruments of knowledge."[89] According to Lenin, these powerful instruments of knowledge are grounded in two interrelated beliefs. First, adapting Engels's claim that our ideas of the real world produce a correct reflection of reality,[90] Lenin introduces into Marxist epistemology his "copy theory" or "theory of reflection." This theory holds that matter is "copied, photographed, and reflected by our sensations"[91]—a statement repeated again and again in Lenin's *Materialism and Empirio-Criticism*. Second, these reflected images, perceived as representations of objective reality, are to be tested by practice—a living human practice that permeates Lenin's theory of knowledge. Not surprisingly, regardless of the more elaborate vision of Marxist epistemology, Lenin, trying to get the subjective knower and the objective world together, accepted without question Marx's dictum that practice is superior to theory. In his *Materialism and Empirio-Criticism*, Lenin states that "the standpoint of life, of practice, should be the first and fundamental in the theory of knowledge."[92] It is also noteworthy that Lenin—just like Marx in the past—considered epistemology a politically partisan science and anyone who did not share his theory of knowledge was labeled as "philosophical scum," guilty of "intellectual poverty and charlatanism."[93]

Georg Lukacs (1885–1971), a more recent central figure in Western Marxism, disagreed with Engels's belief that industry and scientific experiment constitute praxis in the dialectical, philosophical sense, and making the claim that scientific experiment is contemplation at its purest,[94] Lukacs worked his way back to the *Economic and Philosophical Manuscripts of 1844*, concluding that it was Marx who "clearly defined the conditions in which a relation between theory and practice becomes possible." Accordingly, it is only the proletariat as a revolutionary class who can consciously penetrate social reality, and "only when consciousness [of the proletariat] stands in such a relation to reality can theory and practice be united."[95]

Another principal figure in Western Marxism, Karl Korsch (1886–1961), embraced "revolutionary praxis" in the thirties as a "theory of social revolution that comprises all areas of society"[96] and has developed this praxis into a program designed "to acquire objective knowledge by the practical necessities of struggle . . . which commands the Marxists to *subordinate all theoretical knowledge to the end of revolutionary action*."[97] It is quite remarkable that, in the last decade of his life, Korsch radically changed his view on the role of Marxism, declaring that "all attempts to re-establish the Marxist theory as a whole, and its original function as a theory of the working class social revolution, are now reactionary utopias."[98]

Looking at the concept of theory and practice in historical retrospect, it is clear that generations of Marxists who treated theory as a handmaiden of practice ignored or were ignorant of Leonardo da Vinci's attitude toward a shift from theory and science to the belief in the superiority of practice. In da Vinci's view, "Those who fall in love with practice without science are like the sailor who enters a ship without a helm or compass, and who never can be certain whither he is going."[99] Not only was da Vinci's admonition passed over, but despite Hegel's complicated and profound argument for the ultimate unity of theory and practice, in the Marxist tradition this supposed relationship between theory and practice was hardly ever examined in the form of critical arguments or descriptive attributes that would maximize the linkage between theory and practice. In Hegel's view, concepts—in their antithetical as well as their complimentary phase—are of fundamental importance in seeking and expressing the development of knowledge. But this purported unity of theory and practice turned into a peremptory concept, which was unquestioningly accepted and transmitted from generation to generation of Marxists who rarely digressed from the very general framework devised by Marx.

Evidently, Marx did not say much about this concept; but he said enough to make his views on the subject quite attractive to future Marxists, who became so certain of the correlation between theory and practice—with theory serving as a mere complement to practice—that they ceased thinking about the distinctions between intellect and action, settling for unreflective beliefs rather than probing for causal and functional explanations. Apparently, the possibility that a theory may be conjectural, hypothetical, or prescriptive in its quest for practical confirmation never entered the wider range of Marxist discourse. Nor was it of any concern that Aristotle, considering the practical aspects of life, restricted praxis to ethics and politics, carefully separating good praxis (*eupraxia*) from bad praxis (*dyspraxia*). In fact, beginning with Marxists in the nineteenth century and ending with them in the twentieth, the concept of the relation between or unity of theory and practice acquired all the characteristics of a *groupthink enterprise*, which developed into a number of mental fixations, bound to preordained linguistic norms that turned into obstacles to critical thinking and cognitive explanations.

Thus the concept of the unity of theory and practice—"perhaps the proudest boast of Marxism in general"[100]—was deprived of the critical feedback so vital to the communication of ideas that illuminate the contradistinctions between the socio-political sphere and man's real life.

The Unity of Theory and Practice

Interestingly enough, it was Antonio Gramsci who bemoaned the fact that the concept of the unity of theory and practice—which had been in existence almost a century by his time—was still in its initial stage of development. Gramsci, who tried to bring some equilibrium to the relation of theory and practice, placed thought and action within the idea-act-implementation triad in the domain of politics. Assessing the effectiveness of this principle, Gramsci stated that the transitional moments of history identify the intrinsic unity of theory and practice, thus liberating man's power to change and shape reality "through which practice is demonstrated as rational and necessary . . . to achieve the equality of, or equation between, philosophy and politics."[101]

A Marxist theoretician of a lesser stature attempted equally to strike a measure of balance between theory and practice, stating that "theory and practice are high level outgrowths of reciprocal processes of mental enrichment occurring in continual doing and knowing. Acts engender ideas, and ideas engender acts, in an interconnected spiral process involving abstracting-concretizing until ideas attain an initial level of generality, of profundity, of theory, and acts achieve a comprehensiveness in uniformity and individuality of practice"[102] (or perhaps more simply: satisfaction of needs—division of labor—ideas—new ways of satisfying needs, etc.).

In contrast to Western Marxists, Soviet political writers—subservient to the requirements of the party—hardly ever attempted to strike a balanced interaction between theory and practice, or thought and action. Despite their formal insistence on preserving the unity of theory and practice as an integral framework of the Marxist-Leninist doctrine, they diverted this concept from the province of philosophical discourse to a system of rigid, myth-ridden ideological beliefs, virtually canonizing Marx's and Lenin's efforts to subjugate theory to practice.

The Soviet Communist Party subjected Marxist-Leninist theoreticians to heavy-handed directives, centered on efforts to strengthen the superiority of practice, thus legitimizing even impulsive or unreflective action, which usually was glorified in torrents of "propaganda of the word" or "propaganda of the deed." In these circumstances, action, no matter how wrongful or cruel, became its own justification, while theory was called upon to serve as an apology for this action. Moreover, Marxist-Leninist consistency in implementing this policy actually created a schism between theory and practice, dictating the choice of perspectives while distorting, inventing, or suppressing facts in most areas of human behavior.[103] "The accent on practice" as a "necessary condition for society's material and economic progress" was hailed as suitable "for the requirements of social life, and the class struggle."[104]

Curiously, in 1974 a newly revised edition of *The Fundamentals of Marxist-Leninist Philosophy*[105] eliminated the section on "The Unity of Theory and Practice," consigning questions of the class struggle to a separate chapter on "Classes and Class Struggle." Still maintaining that "the basis of knowledge . . . is *in social historical practice*,"[106] Soviet theoreticians declared that the "most important principle of Marxism-Leninism is the bonding of theory and practice" (without explaining the meaning of "bonding'" or how it differs from "unity"), designed to test "theoretical propositions in practice" and to develop "theory on the basis of generalization of practical experience."[107] Thus theory was no longer a theory *for* practice but was transformed into a theory *of* practice[108]—a practice leading, frequently, to savage activism which, in the process of bringing about a new and "better" society, produced damnable results.

With theory no longer delving into the complex facts of man and society, theory ceased to explain what the world is like or what its truthful representation is. This state of affairs was characterized by a lack of a disinterested striving for truth for its own sake, and because of the strong predominance of Marxist-Leninist "truths"—based on a sharply reduced role of theory so that it concerned vague and largely utopian socialist aims—these "truths" contributed to a radically distorted view of Soviet reality in the educational system; in textbooks, speeches, literature, journals, newspapers; and in the broadcast media.[109] But one of the most blatant distortions of truth had taken place in the corruption of democratic principles—a topic rarely analyzed at length in the annals of Sovietology—which is the subject matter of the next chapter.

Notes

1. Cited in Erich Fromm, *Marx's Concept of Man* (New York: Frederick Ungar Publishing Co., 1960), 259.

2. Karl Marx and Friedrich Engels, *Basic Writings on Politics and Philosophy*, ed. Lewis S. Feuer (Garden City, N.Y.: Anchor Books, 1959), 244. Henceforth referred to as *Basic Writings*.

3. Ludwig Feuerbach's *The Essence of Christianity*, published in 1841, greatly impressed and influenced Marx's generation.

4. *Basic Writings*, 243.

5. Ibid.

6. Robert C. Tucker, ed., *The Marx-Engels Reader* (New York: Norton, 1972), 3–5.

7. Karl Marx and Friedrich Engels, *The German Ideology* (New York: International Publishers, 1969), 13–14.

8. Ibid., 7; Marx reiterated a similar view as late as 1880. See Derek Sayer, *Marx's Method* (Atlantic Highlands, N.J.: Humanities Press, 1979), 157.

9. Ibid., 28.

10. Marx got the idea from Hegel and Rousseau. For a more thorough analysis of this aphorism, see John Plamenatz, *German Marxism and Russian Communism* (London: Longmans, Green and Co., 1954), 14–17.

11. C. E. M. Joad, *Guide to Philosophy* (London: V. Gollancz Ltd., 1936), 475.

12. Marx and Engels, *The German Ideology*, 34.

13. *Basic Writings*, 243. Marx's scathing anti-Semitic remarks about Lassale ("Nigger-Jew," "Baron Itzick," etc.) are well documented. In a letter written in 1879 from Ramsgate, Marx tells Engels that there were "many Jews and bedbugs hereabouts." For more outbursts of a similar kind, see Saul K. Padover, *The Letters of Karl Marx* (Englewood Cliffs, N.J.: Prentice-Hall, 1979).

14. Joseph Clark, "Marx and the Jews: Another View," *Dissent* (Winter 1981): 74.

15. *Basic Writings*, 243.

16. *The Letters of Karl Marx*, 30–31.

17. Ibid., 32.

18. *The German Ideology*, 7.

19. Cited in Wallace K. Ferguson and Geoffrey Bruun, *A Survey of Western Civilization* (Boston: Houghton Mifflin & Co., 1962), 576.

20. Francis Bacon, *Novum Organum,* in *Man and the Universe: The Philosophers of Science*, ed. Saxe Commins & Robert N. Linscott (New York: Random House, 1947), 78.

21. *The German Ideology*, 13–14.

22. Alfred North Whitehead, *Adventures of Ideas* (New York: Macmillan, 1933), 125.

23. The pragmatic, the instrumental, and the semantic theories of truth are "products" of more recent times—the end of the nineteenth and the beginning decades of the twentieth centuries.

24. William Wallace, *The Logic of Hegel* (New York and London: Oxford University Press, 1968), 52–53.

25. *Basic Writings*, 243. Emphasis added.

26. Ibid.

27. *Novum Organum*, 78.

28. Karl Marx, *Capital: A Critique of Political Economy* (New York: Modern Library, 1906), 197.

29. Ibid., 23.

30. For a good, if somewhat one-sided, reference source on the "flirtation" between Marxists and pragmatists, see George Novack, *Pragmatism Versus Marxism* (New York: Pathfinder Press, 1975).

31. John Dewey, *Logic: The Theory of Inquiry,* vol. 12 in *The Later Works, 1925-53* (Carbondale and Edwardsville: Southern Illinois University Press, 1986).

32. *The Philosophy of John Dewey*, ed. Joseph Ratner (New York: Henry Holt and Co., 1928), 240.
33. Dewey, *Logic*, 108.
34. Ibid., 343.
35. Bertrand Russell, "Dewey's New Logic," in *The Philosophy of John Dewey*, ed. Arthur Schlipp (Evanston, Ill.: Northwestern University Press, 1939), 143. A similar appraisal of instrumentalism may be found in Bertrand Russell, *Freedom Versus Organization* (New York: W.W. Norton & Co., 1934), 191–92.
36. Quoted in Novack, *Pragmatism versus Marxism*, 272.
37. Cited in Max Eastman, *Marxism: Is It a Science?* (New York: W.W. Norton & Co., 1940), 342.
38. Cited in Nicholas Lobkowitz, *Theory and Practice: History of a Concept from Aristotle to Marx* (Notre Dame, Ind.: University Press of Notre Dame, 1967), 298 and 240.
39. Bertrand Russell, *A History of Western Philosophy* (New York: Simon & Schuster, 1945), 822.
40. In all fairness, it must be stated that, in his later years, Sidney Hook argued that Marxism espouses a kind of vulgar pragmatism.
41. Cited in Harry Prosch, *The Genesis of Twentieth Century Philosophy* (New York: Anchor Books, 1966), 353.
42. Dewey, *Logic*, 181.
43. However, Marx's reverence for science and his aspiration to scientificity stand in sharp contrast to the anti-rationalist strain in contemporary neo-Marxism, (e.g., Herbert Marcuse's *Eros and Civilization* and *One-Dimensional Man*), especially in "postmodern" and "deconstructionist" attempts to read Nietzsche and Heidegger into Marx.
44. Karl Marx, *The Grundrisse*, ed. and trans. by David McLellan (New York: Harper and Row, 1971), General Introduction.
45. *Basic Writings*, 7.
46. Kenneth Boulding, in his *A Primer of Social Dynamics* (New York: The Free Press, 1970), proves that endowing history with dialectical qualities is inconsistent with actual processes of history.
47. According to David Felix, Marx's phrase in the *Manifesto*—that "working men have no fatherland, saved the proletariat from nationalism . . . [which] would mean the end of all national hostilities." David Felix, *Marx as Politician* (Carbondale and Edwardsville: Southern Illinois University Press, 1983), 155–56.
48. Marx considered religion as a manifestation of man's historical imperfection. Engels, however, wrote extensively on this subject, exploring the interplay of politics and religion in his works *The Peasant War in Germany* and *On the History of Early Christianity*. Prestigious studies on war and the human race, such as Quincy Wright, *A Study of War* (Chicago: The University of Chicago Press, 1970); L. L. Bernard, *A Study of War and its Causes* (New York: Henry Holt and Co., 1944); and Michael Howard, *The Causes of*

Wars (Cambridge: Harvard University Press, 1983), hardly pay any attention to Marx's concept of class struggle in the classification of the causes of war. In ascribing a momentous significance to the concept of class struggle in international relations, Marx disregarded the powerful element of nationalism. Even in Marx's times, it was generally recognized that once a nation—though composed of antagonistic classes—is built and consolidated, it acquires an autonomous drive of its own. It is not only language but other characteristics—e.g., territory, ethnic origin, national values, self-assertion, and national pride—that are generally unaffected by class divisions.

49. *Basic Writings*, 244.

50. In 1872, twenty-four years later, Marx conceded in a speech to the Hague Congress that "countries such as America and England" and possibly "Holland, where the workers may attain their goals by peaceful means," would not undergo such a revolution. Cited in Jon Elster's *Making Sense of Marx* (Cambridge: Cambridge University Press, 1985), 446.

51. *Basic Writings*, 245.

52. Ibid., 28.

53. *The Marx-Engels Reader*, 363–73.

54. Ibid., 366.

55. Ibid., 367–68.

56. Ibid., 368.

57. Ibid.

58. Ibid.

59. Ibid., 371.

60. Cited in Lewis S. Feuer, *Marx and the Intellectuals* (New York: Anchor Books, 1969), 16.

61. *Literaturnaia Gazeta* (June 14, 1989): 3.

62. It is not at all surprising that people in the former Soviet Union, demonstrating against the rule of the Communist Party, carried signs with the inscription "SEVENTY YEARS ON THE ROAD TO NOWHERE!"

63. Shlomo Avinieri, in his magisterial work *The Social and Political Thought of Karl Marx* (New York and Cambridge: Cambridge University Press, 1968), notes that "Marx's pre-1848 and post-1848 attitudes differ only with regard to the scope of capitalist development" (253). And he adds that "with all the differences between Marx, and Soviet, Leninist Communism, Leninism would have been inconceivable without Marx."

64. Karl Marx and Friedrich Engels, *Selected Works,* vol. 2 (Moscow: Foreign Languages Publishing House, 1962), 485.

65. *Writings of the Young Marx on Philosophy and Society*, ed. and trans. Lloyd D. Easton and Kurt Guddat (Garden City, N.Y.: Doubleday & Co., 1967), 2.

66. Karl Marx, *Economic and Philosophical Manuscripts of 1844* (New York: International Publishers, 1964).

67. Ernst Bloch, *On Karl Marx* (New York: Herder and Herder, 1971), 15 and 23. See also Fromm, *Marx's Concept of Man*, 70; and Howard L. Par-

sons, *Humanism and Marx's Thought* (Springfield, Ill.: Charles. C. Thomas, 1971).

68. Karl Marx and Friedrich Engels, *Collected Works*, ed. D. Rjazanov and V. Adoratsky (Frankfurt, 1927), generally known as MEGA.

69. Lobkowitz, *Theory and Practice*, 408.

70. Saul K. Padover, *Karl Marx: An Intimate Biography* (New York: McGraw Hill Book Co., 1978), 190–91.

71. David McLellan, *Karl Marx: His Life and Thought* (New York: Harper and Row, 1973), 128.

72. Herbert Marcuse, *Soviet Marxism: A Critical Analysis* (New York: Columbia University Press, 1958), 147; and Leonard Krieger, "Marx and Engels as Historians," *Journal of the History of Ideas* XIV, no. 3 (June, 1953): 396.

73. Tom Bottomore, ed., *Dictionary of Marxist Thought* (Cambridge: Harvard University Press, 1983), 387. Henceforth referred to as *Dictionary*.

74. Cited in Franz Marek, *Philosophy of World Revolution* (London: Lawrence & Wishart, 1969), 22.

75. *Dictionary*, 386.

76. Cited in *Karl Marx: The Red Prussian* by Leopold Schwarzshield (New York: Universal Library, Grosset & Dunlap, 1947), 80.

77. In this, as in many things, Marx relied on but transformed Hegel's dialectic. In Hegel's view, theoretical contradictions that appear "tragic" in their own time—the opposition between Antigone and Creon, for example, or Socrates and the Athenian polis—could be resolved by history through a praxis that would produce a society in which the relationship between the individual and the state would be decisively altered. Alexander Kojeve, "Tyranny and Wisdom," in Leo Strauss, *On Tyranny*, eds. Victor Gourevitch and Michael S. Roth (New York: Free Press, 1963), 135–76.

78. Curiously enough, Engels, who is praised by some students of Marxism as a military "expert," somehow greatly underestimated the violent extent of revolutionary street battles in a preface to Marx's *Class Struggles in France*, stating that "street fighting presented certain *inconveniences* and that the faithful need not necessarily feel committed to it." Cited in Joseph A. Schumpeter, *Capitalism, Socialism and Democracy* (New York: Harper Torchbooks, 1947), 346. Emphasis added.

79. *Dictionary*, 387.

80. Ibid.

81. Cited in V.I. Lenin, *Materialism and Empirio-Criticism* (Moscow: Foreign Languages Publishing House, 1952), 105.

82. Ironically, under the Soviet regime, "ideas" proved generally stronger than—and often incorrigible by—practice. Practical failure did not lead to the correction of ideas and theories, because censorship—justified by the system's claim to "scientificity"—prevented these failures from becoming fully public (consider the environmental disaster of the Aral Sea or the suppression of various air crashes and nuclear accidents). Boris Pasternak summed it up most succinctly: "Collectivization was an erroneous and unsuccessful mea-

sure and it was impossible to admit the error. To conceal the failure people had to be cured, by every means of terrorism, of the habit of thinking and judging for themselves, and forced to see what didn't exist, to assert the very opposite of what their eyes told them" (*Doctor Zhivago* [New York: Pantheon, 1958], 507).

83. Marx, speaking about the relation of theory and practice, never used the expression "the unity of theory and practice."

84. Georgi Plekhanov, *Selected Philosophical Works* (Moscow: Progress Publishers, 1980), vol. IV, 346 and 355.

85. Cited in Vladimir Akimov, *Dilemmas of Russian Marxism 1805-1903*, ed. Jonathan Frankel (New York and Cambridge: Cambridge University Press, 1969), 285.

86. Cited in Sidney Hook, *Marx and the Marxists* (Princeton, N.J.: D. Van Nostrand Co., 1955), 61.

87. V. I. Lenin, *Collected Works*, vol. 21 (Moscow: Progress Publishers, 1961), 218–19.

88. V. I. Lenin, *Selected Works*, vol. II (New York: International Publishers, 1967), 168–69.

89. Ibid., vol. I, 43.

90. Karl Marx and Friedrich Engels, *Selected Works* (New York: International Publishers, 1968), 605.

91. Cited in James P. Scanlan, *Marxism in the USSR* (Ithaca, N.Y.: Cornell University Press, 1985), 144.

92. *Materialism and Empirio-Criticism*, 141.

93. Cited in Nikolai Valentinov, *Encounters with Lenin* (London: Oxford University Press, 1968), 246.

94. *Dictionary*, 387.

95. Georg Lukacs, *History and Class Consciousness* (Cambridge, Mass.: MIT Press, 1971), 3.

96. Karl Korsch, *Marxism and Philosophy* (New York: Modern Reader, 1970), 70.

97. Karl Korsch, *Three Essays on Marxism* (New York: Monthly Review Press, 1971), 68–70.

98. *Dictionary*, 264.

99. Cited in W. T. Jones, *A History of Western Philosophy* (New York: Harcourt, Brace & World, 1952), 593.

100. Robert L. Heilbroner, *Marxism: For and Against* (New York: W.W. Norton & Co., 1980), 79.

101. *Selections from the Prison Notebooks of Antonio Gramsci* (New York: International Publishers, 1971), 356, 365.

102. Ira Gollobin, *Dialectical Materialism* (New York: Petras Press, 1986), 378.

103. See n. 82.

104. *Fundamentals of Marxism-Leninism* (Moscow: Foreign Languages Publishing House, 1963), 94.

105. *The Fundamentals of Marxist-Leninist Philosophy* (Moscow: Progress Publishers, 1974).
106. Ibid., 217.
107. Ibid., 661.
108. T. A. Jackson, *Dialectics* (New York: International Publishers, 1936), 582; excerpted from Nicolai Bukharin's "Theory and Practice from the Standpoint of Dialectical Materialism."
109. A substantially altered preliminary version of this chapter, "The Unity of Theory and Practice in Historical Perspective," appeared in *Studies in Soviet Thought* 41 (1991): 173–205 (© 1991, by Sigmund Krancberg).

3

The Corruption of Democratic Principles

> For the past two decades Soviet society has remained essentially the political-economic system first created under Stalin, with the one important modification that the use of terror diminished and changed in character.
>
> Victor Zaslavsky (1982)[1]

The structural framework of the totalitarian-bureaucratic model is not only coincidental with the reality of things in the neo-Stalinist state; it is also a systematic clarification of the hierarchical differentiation of the ruling elite that exercised a high degree of control over Soviet society. And yet, necessary and consistent as these formulations appear in Chapter 1, we must go beyond them in order to explore the goals-means relationships reflected in the horizontal concepts that embrace the totality of coercive measures designed to atomize Soviet society—a society forced into an artificial state of permanent mobilization of manpower and resources "entrusted" with the building of a classless Communist society.

For a better understanding of the determinate sphere of operations in the totalitarian-bureaucratic environment, we may compare the horizontal concepts to ever-widening concentric circles of propaganda surrounding the helpless individual[2]—the "common man" usually extolled in the official Soviet press as the "builder of communism" but who, in reality, was deprived of independent judgment and personal integrity. While effectively barred from the decision-making process, this common man was subjected to relentless pressures of ideological indoctrination, almost round-the-clock propaganda, and outright intimidation. With the reserves of revolutionary enthusiasm largely exhausted, the Communist leaders transformed force into right and obedience into duty, demanding compliance and loyalty, justifying their rule in the name of a system that was supposedly "continually improving, expanding and comprising new components with the increasing complexity of building socialism and communism."³

Against the vision of a promised ideal society to be built in the not-too-distant future, the totalitarian bureaucratic apparatus represented a gangster-style politics of will and might with the Communist rulers free to determine the policies and the course of action howsoever they decided. Needless to say, this kind of "revolutionary" politics—a politics shaped according to Marxist-Leninist principles—overstepped the limits of sound and responsible political thought and practice essential to the functioning of an enlightened, civilized society. Nevertheless, some Western Sovietologists overlooked the darker side of Soviet political life, claiming that "behaviors elicited by Marxism-Leninism analytically fit conventional social scientific definitions . . . [and that] Marxism and even Leninism need not be seen as *congenitally deformed.*"⁴

In still another respect, despite the well-known fact that "obkom [Regional Committee of the Party] first secretaries behaved like the 'feudal lords' in the provinces,"⁵ a prominent Western Sovietologist attempted to reassess the role of the Communist Party in a more favorable light:

> Public opinion polls in recent years suggest that ordinary Soviet citizens—or at least the Slavic majority—are even more conservative than some segments of the ruling elite. The importance of this deep-rooted conservatism . . . compels us to rethink the whole relationship between the party-state and society in the Soviet Union, including the political system's remarkable *stability* despite large and persistent problems. It again suggests that Sovietologists and other observers, by failing to perceive anything organic in that relationship, still overemphasize coercive aspects of official Soviet politics and policy while underestimating consensual ones.⁶

It is not an exaggeration to say that, in the controlled environment of totalitarian politics, public polls conducted by homegrown sociologists carried as much weight as the deceptive practice of Soviet "elections." Still, if some Sovietologists have distanced themselves from the "coercive aspects of official Soviet politics and policy"—a very misleading approach to begin with—another "area specialist," David Lane, tried to find some justification for the coercive character of the neo-Stalinist state. Portraying the Communist empire as a "modernizing industrial society" that is "in many ways like other industrial societies," beset by "problems of 'directed' social change," of a "command or state socialist society,"⁷ David Lane states:

> The apparatus of government under state socialism cannot merely be characterized as "bureaucratic," "a bureaucratic deformation" or "dictatorial." The lack of popular control of the state, or absence of organs of people's power which replace the state, must be attributed to two features in the evolution of these societies. First, in the international context, emerging socialist societies have been confronted with militarily powerful capitalist states; Soviet military expenditure is a response to the threat to USSR's political integrity. Second, a popular participant culture may arise only on the basis of a high level of political competence on the part of the masses. . . . The low level of the political and social consciousness of the [Soviet] masses, the lack of a deep socialist ethos, therefore, become a barrier to the development of a socialist consciousness.[8]

Throughout his book, David Lane fails to explain what he means by "a deep socialist ethos," and he is equally vague about "the political and ideological apparatuses of the state," which may not have been "hegemonic in their role of creating socialist relationships" but may have had "to compromise with the forces of coercion."[9] If—ignoring the brute facts of Soviet reality—we take this statement about "the political and ideological apparatuses of the state" at face value, it is clear that Lane unwittingly aspires to provide an expression of sympathy with the Soviet leaders, who were allegedly inclined to introduce democracy to the Soviet people but could not do it because of "the low level of the political and social consciousness of the [Soviet] masses." It is obvious that Lane fails to take into account the historical record of the neo-Stalinist leaders, their simultaneous idealization of the masses coupled with ambitious and, at times, vicious struggles for power. Furthermore, their frequent abuses of power, carried out with a sense of self-confidence and self-righteousness, generated ideological distortions of reality, dogmatism, and duplicity in whichever ways the dictates of power seemed to demand.

It is also a fact that Soviet leaders, uncurbed by any countervailing authority and free of any constraints exercised by publicly controlled agencies (civil society as we know it in the West did not exist in the Soviet Union), were driven by the "delight in power; the cancer of power," which the Polish writer Tadeusz Konwicki defines as the essence of rule in Communist party-states.[10] This "delight in power" turned into an intoxication with power,[11] particularly when arbitrary policies and savage actions became inextricably confused with Marxist-Leninist principles. It was Bertrand Russell who observed: "I am persuaded that this intoxication [with power] is the greatest threat of our time, and that any philosophy which, however unintentionally, contributes to it, is increasing the danger of vast social disaster."[12]

However negligent in gathering evidence on the widespread abuses of power frequently utilized by Soviet authorities to conceal the blatant failures of the totalitarian-bureaucratic system, Sovietologists have been even more neglectful of the malicious corruption of democratic principles in the political environment of the neo-Stalinist state. In some cases it was blamed on Marx's supposedly ill-explained account of the transition to socialism, although Marx and Engels are quite clear on the need for a dictatorship of the proletariat to consolidate the gains of the revolution. In other cases, the fault was a misreading of the works of Marx and Engels, as demonstrated in the assertion by a renowned social scientist who states that "*the dictatorship of the proletariat* is a phrase seldom used by Marx and Engels."[13] Contrary to this assertion, the Subject Index (*Sachregister*) of the *Collected Works of Karl Marx and Friedrich Engels,* published by Dietz Verlag in Berlin (1984), cites eighty-three entries under the heading of the "Diktatur des Proletariats." The same social scientist proclaims that "Marx conceived of proletarian government as being, from the very beginning, *more truly democratic and liberal* than anything known to bourgeois Europe."[14] Surprisingly, a few paragraphs later, he takes notice of Marx's predilection for a "strong central government so badly needed by a revolutionary power," conjoined with Marx's admiration of "the Jacobins of the great French Revolution for setting aside the first revolutionary constitution, which had given wide powers to elected local authorities."[15]

In another instance, trying to divorce Marx's "project" from Soviet "authoritarianism," the Sovietologist David W. Lovell states that

> to Marx's ill-explained notion of the transition to socialism Lenin brought only an understanding of the imperatives of the dictatorship of the proletariat, a concept he revived and exploited masterfully in his debates against other Marxists. Marx's was a sin of omission, not commission. Lenin supplied the theoretical foundations for Soviet authoritarianism; Marx's contribution to them was not decisive. While there are many cogent reasons for rejecting Marx's project as a panacea for society's ills, the project's direct and necessary association with Soviet illiberalism is not one of them.[16]

In contrast to Lovell—who studiously abstains from the use of the term "totalitarianism" throughout his book—the late and famous Soviet dissident A. Amalrik clearly connects Marx's project to Lenin's onslaught on liberty and democracy before and after the October Revolution. Thus Amalrik declares: "Lenin may have forced Marx, but the responsibility for Leninism and Stalinism is intellectually rooted in Marx. . . . The *whole* Marx leads, directly or indirectly, to Lenin."[17]

Equally significant is the following pronouncement of two distinguished political scientists D. J. Manning and T. J. Robinson: "It is our view that without the doctrines of Marxism there could have been no Bolshevik party, and without a command of the Marxist vocabulary Lenin would not have been able to convince its members that he was their authentic leader."[18]

But nowhere is this connection more clearly revealed than in Lenin's statement of September 11, 1917:

> We do not pretend that Marx or Marxists know the road to socialism in all its concreteness. That is nonsense. We know the *direction* [emphasis added] of the road, we know what class forces lead to it, but concretely, practically, this will be shown by the *experience of the millions* when they undertake to act.[19]

A somewhat more meaningful assessment is adapted by Sir John Maynard, a recognized authority on the history of modern Russia, when he states that Marx "furnished the philosophy, and in some degree the technique, of revolution; and he furnished certain principles which might guide the builders of a part at least of the new temple."[20]

It is evident that Marx's revolutionary principles—accepted by Communists as ageless truths—provided direction and guidance for Lenin who, in overstepping the limits of the human condition, shared with Marx his strong revulsion against democratic and liberal principles. What is generally overlooked is that this feeling of strong revulsion, part of an unnatural contempt for democracy, was instrumental in creating a Marxist-Leninist nonprincipled praxis of power that claimed justification in a logic of ideological and social domination.

Now, with the collapse of communism, it is worthwhile to go back to the roots of this nonprincipled praxis which led to the suppression by the Bolsheviks of political movements beginning with liberalism and ending with anarchism.

There is a celebrated and influential argument to the effect that, if language and thought are intimately related, then we must assume that we live in an interpreted world in which straightforward facts, in their direct coincidence with reality, are consigned to the background regardless of their occurrence.[21] According to this line of reasoning, descriptive and prescriptive interpretations are advanced as the dominant currency of philosophical or political concern, and facts—in all their significance—may be viewed only from a range of perspectives related to their condition or existence. In its most radical form, this body of knowledge, known as *perspectivism*, claims that it speaks of seeing the same thing from different vantage points that are ascertained by a highly complex intellectual process of interpretation, filling in "the blank surface of reality with the longitudes and parallels of concepts"[22]—concepts that are mere semblances of reality.

It is obvious that in the attempt to arrive at an explanation of appearance and reality, perspectivism gives rise to controversial questions regarding our knowledge of facts in their concrete and original character—a knowledge that embraces the distinctive determination of identity and difference in an intelligible setting. Still, dispensing with a detailed evaluation of the positive and negative aspects of perspectivism—an enterprise extraneous to the purpose of this study—it is not hazardous to infer that, in order to ensure intellectual integrity and a validity of meaning in applying the perspectival approach, we must constantly make provisions for a well-balanced and conscientious endeavor focused on every point of reference in relation to distance, depth, and relevance of a given "fact." Under no circumstances should our observations be restricted to one specific vantage point or to one aspect singled out for preferential treatment to the exclusion of other qualities or features of paramount importance.

As if neglecting this requirement for a well-balanced and conscientious approach, a number of scholars, intent on elevating Marx to a more respectable reputation, attribute to him a lifelong devotion to democracy, and in line with this "theory," they attempt to portray Marx as a humanist and thinker in the mainstream of Western tradition. And, indeed, when we inquire into and seek to understand the nature of these unfounded claims, we find in our research only one ill-defined source well-known to serious students of Marxism—a source readily obtained from a few isolated pages in the *Critique of Hegel's Philosophy of Right*,[23] in which the young Marx speaks in positive but broad, general terms about democracy, constitutionality, and religion.

Despite the fact that this categorization of Marx as a democrat and humanist ignores the sharp contradictions dividing the concerns of the young Marx from the revolutionary posture of the more mature Marx, there exists nonetheless a group of friendly critics who, according to the late Sidney Hook, have jointly heralded the "second coming of Karl Marx."[24] One such critic, Joseph O'Malley, asserted that "there appears to be no basis for the view that the young and the old Marx represent two distinct periods in which his doctrinal principles, his theoretical and practical concerns and his intellectual positions were radically opposed."[25]

With unrestrained enthusiasm and completely disregarding Marx's resolve to effect a violent transformation of society,[26] these friendly critics have proclaimed Marx as the defender of democracy, ignoring the fact that, in later life, Marx labeled representative and participatory democracy as "democratic nonsense" and "political windbaggery."[27] This kind of grandiloquence is ignored by Maximilien Rubel—an outstanding Marxist scholar according to some academicians—who declared that Marx was "a revolutionary communist only in theory, while he was a bourgeois democrat in practice."[28] Apparently aware that this contradictory statement represents a denial of the artful construct known in Marxist terminology as the "unity of theory and practice," Maximilien Rubel adds that this portrayal of Marx is "after all, the logical consequence of his dialectical method."[29] It seems that Rubel is grappling with shadows, unconcerned with the fact that reconciling two contradictories in a dialectical synthesis is outside the framework of consistency and is at odds with experience—an experience that, in this case, ends in a disturbing paradox.

And indeed, in the words of a notable Western Marxist, the dialectic "yields a rich harvest for the imagination, but a scanty one for exact analysis."[30] That the dialectical method or the dialectic is beyond the reach of exact analysis is a view shared equally by most Western scholars, represented at their best by the Austrian philosopher Ernst Topitsch, who offered the following critique of Marxist dialectics: "The question of what dialectics really is, what advantages it possesses over other ways of looking at things, has not been answered."[31]

Even more characteristic of the questionable validity of Marxist dialectics or the dialectical method is the generally recognized fact that this method is a kind of pseudologic, which can neither be verified nor refuted.[32] Of course, it follows that, if dialectics or the dialectical method is beyond verification, then this dialectic can be manipulated at will.[33] But for Maximilien Rubel, Marx, newly refurbished against the backdrop of the dialectic, appears as the lover of humanity and as the "passionate observer and stern judge of deeds and men, pronouncing his verdict in conformity with certain norms and values underlying the *Weltanschauung* he built up in the first five or six years of his ideological formation."[34]

In another example, the late Erich Fromm refused to draw a demarcation line between the young and the mature Marx, declaring that

"Marx was one among the great humanist philosophers who, like the humanists from the Renaissance up to those of our day, have stressed the ideas that all social arrangements must serve the growth and unfolding of man."³⁵ Proclaiming the rebirth of humanism rooted in the Marxist doctrine (is it part of humanism to advocate the social and physical liquidation of entire classes?), Fromm, through the use of euphemisms, managed to reverse the meaning of such concepts as "social arrangements" and "the growth and unfolding of man" into Marxist notions that stand as substitutes for the unchallengeable right to enforce a Communist blueprint on the new social order and, true to Marx's goal, to establish this new social order by violent means.

It seems that the writers who desire to "save" Marx share a propensity for making pronouncements in place of thought—a propensity that shows a lack of clarity in their manner of expression, as exemplified in the following passage: "The time has come for a post-modern interpretation of Marx, one that helps to explain the limits to this radical humanism."³⁶ The author, in this instance, in his attempt to prove that one can be a Marxist without being a Communist, forgets his statement on "the limits of Marx's radical humanism" and offers in the same paragraph this new interpretation: "Marx strove for a *unified humanistic perspective* in his writings, and hence he should not be considered an unequivocal advocate of a Stalinesque system of hierarchical 'command planning' that coerces and alienates the citizenry."³⁷

But the question of Marx's guilt in advocating a Stalinesque system is not at issue. The stated purpose of this study is to reestablish the link between Marx and Lenin—a subject matter largely neglected or belittled by students of the Soviet phenomenon—to search for evidence of the "totalitarian embryo" in Marx's writings that set the stage for the twentieth century totalitarianism entrenched in the Communist social order of the Soviet Union. In his analytical inquiry into the political and philosophical framework of Karl Marx's life and thought, Leszek Kolakowski—a recognized authority on the main currents of Marxism—stated in one of his essays: "Despotic socialism arose from many historical circumstances, the Marxist tradition among them."³⁸

It is noteworthy that conditions changed so radically as a result of the colossal failure and political bankruptcy of the Soviet experiment that the lived experience of a devout Marxist shows serious difficulties in the process of theoretical and political reorientation. In this instance, yesterday's Marxist tries to cling to a Marxist tradition that defies the logic of history. Thus Sidney Hook, who was actively involved in leftist politics in the 1930s, states in one of his later works:

"The conception of the dictatorship of the [Soviet Communist] Party over the proletariat, confirmed by the whole history of the Soviet Union, marks an absolute break with all the democratic traditions in Marxism."[39]

Even twenty years later, Sidney Hook still claimed that the Bolshevization of Marx represented a betrayal of the Marxian ethos, reluctantly conceding that "there was something in Marx's attitude towards the philosophy of the Enlightenment which prepared the way for it."[40] As Hook explains it, this shortcoming was due to Marx's interpretation of natural and human rights in terms of a pure ideology—an ideology reduced to personal gains reflected in the class egoism of civil society. Needless to say, Marx's concept of civil society (as well as his contempt for civil society) was afforded a rather biased, narrow definition within the broad category of a society beset by the burgeoning capitalism of the nineteenth century. As Hook noted correctly, Marx's portrait of this society ignores the essence of natural or human rights with its legal foundations, thereby constituting a decisive step in the restraint of excesses of power.[41]

What Marxists and Crypto-Marxists overlook is the fact that the mature Marx tended toward fanaticism in his dedication to political concepts and principles—a mental attitude alien to a democratic outlook.[42] Moreover, that democracy is important in a purely symbolic sense to the socialist project is clearly demonstrated by writers who muddle the distinctions between the young and the older Marx—writers who use careless language and free indirect citation, taking for granted that Karl Marx in his more mature years still adhered to the democratic views of his youth.

However, if we wish to evaluate correctly the young Marx's views on democracy, we must turn to his reflections on democracy, expressed in the context of his *Economic and Philosophical Manuscripts of 1844*,[43] and explore how these views radically changed in his more mature years—a change in principles that guided Lenin in his revolutionary activity leading to the October Revolution.

In taking up the problems of a community that governs itself, Marx proclaims that "democracy is the truth of monarchy; monarchy is not the truth of democracy."[44] This awkward epigram—a far cry from a normative definition of democracy—is rendered in the idiom of the Hegelian dialectic wherein two different and even incompatible meanings are supposed to dissolve in polarized abstractions, illuminating each other as opposites. Thus, without a clear taxonomic approach, one societal arrangement—democracy—is pronounced as eternal truth, while monarchy—which is democracy's antithesis—is declared as a perversion of democracy. It is noteworthy that the young Marx is satisfied with the high-sounding symbolic expressions, making no attempt to arrive at a clear, definite interpretation or explanation of the political processes under one or the other socio-political arrangement.

In a somewhat similar fashion, Marx declares that "democracy is content and form" while "monarchy *might* be only form, but falsifies the content."[45] Here again, Marx speaks of democracy in terms of an esoteric truth stripped of its basic principles and issues, reducing its plurality of viewpoints and its elements of tolerance to sheer dialectical speculations. The young Marx shows his almost total dependence on Hegel's mode of thought by referring to the latter's *Science of Logic*, in which the importance and inseparability of the categories of *content* and *form* are represented in the practical and rational sense, reflecting the transition from the category of *appearance* to the category of *actuality*.[46] To be sure, the young Marx knew his Hegel; but the statement that "democracy is content and form" is so abstract and remote from social realities that it says virtually nothing. Furthermore, Marx states that "democracy can be conceived in its own terms"[47] but never explains the real meaning of these terms or their relation to political principles. If, in his "analysis," Marx treats democracy as if it meant something very definite—without intimating that behind the concept of democracy is a wealth of conceivable forms in which the people may participate in the orderly process of responsible government—what are the actual political aspects or principles implicated in the case of democracy as related to a social content? Apparently, the young Marx is at a loss for reasonable explanations of all these aspects of democracy.

It is obvious that Marx's method of political analysis in the *Critique* is mainly postulated in isolated comments that lack determinate meaning. It seems that what obstructed Marx's insight into the specific distinctions between democracy and monarchy was his superficial knowledge of the workings of a democratic form of government. Democratic institutions were few and mostly short-lived in the Germany of Marx's time, and the Hegelian dialectic in which Marx was schooled encouraged a discounting of political forms in favor of historical process. Apparently, Marx had difficulties in visualizing a workable democratic form of government, which sets itself goals and then seeks the best means to achieve them in a dynamic political process based on a free and mutual interchange of conceptions and beliefs in an atmosphere of tolerance. In his dimension of thought, Marx never elucidated the vision of a society that provides a forum for open discussion and the articulation of practical political methods decided upon by conscious coordination and design.

It is likewise certain that, when the *1844 Manuscripts*—which Marx never intended to publish—were written, Marx considered himself Hegel's disciple, despite his participation in forging the anti-feudal program of the Young Hegelians. It was Hegel who called the state "divine" and "absolutely rational," and it was Hegel who did not hesitate to elevate the state to the actualization of the ethical ideal—a political structure in which the common citizens are categorized merely as *accidents*. Therefore it is hardly surprising that, in consequence, Hegel defines the state as a "great architectonic structure" and a "hieroglyph of reason which reveals itself in actuality,"[48] crowning these statements with the famous phrase "The March of God in the world, that's what the state is."[49] Thus Hegel elevates reason to an absolute trust in the reality of things—a reason that cannot be detached from the divine, in a truly constitutive category identified as "a self-determining sovereign will, as final decision."[50]

However, as if in an afterthought, reflecting on the reality of the ethical and communal life in the limited, narrow world of the Prussian despotic monarchy, Hegel warns that the state "stands on earth, and so in the sphere of caprice, chance and error, and bad behavior may disfigure it in many respects."[51]

It seems that the young Marx, studying carefully *Hegel's Philosophy of Right*, had probably taken notice of Hegel's warning and, in turn, attempted in general terms in his *Critique* not only to overcome Hegel's philosophical and political idealism but also to bring man and the state closer together, that is, to enter man and the state into a relationship that would be free of conflict and contradiction. But for this new bond to assert itself in more than a mere formal connection, circumstances have to be created in which the conscious absorption of society by the individual has to take place in the free recognition by each individual of himself as a bearer of political and legal rights that are guaranteed by a democratic state. Accordingly, it is sufficient to recall what Sir Isaiah Berlin, a scholar of great probity and insight, has to say about Marx and democracy:

> The manifestoes, professions of faith and programs of action to which he appended his name, contain scarcely any references to moral progress, eternal justice, the equality of man, the rights of individuals or nations, the liberty of conscience, the fight for civilization, and other such phrases which were the stock in trade (and had once genuinely embodied ideals of the democratic movements of his time; he looked

upon these as so much worthless cant, indicating confusion of thought and ineffectiveness in action).[52]

However we may judge his theoretical shortcomings in the appreciation of democracy as a political theory or program, Marx also encountered obstacles in disengaging himself from Hegel's highly technical vocabulary, which constitutes the most original feature of Hegel's philosophical system. It is hardly necessary to stress this point when we evaluate Marx's argument advanced against Hegel's view of the state: "Hegel proceeds from the state and makes man subjectivized. Democracy proceeds from man and makes the state into man objectivized."[53] In simpler terms, this means that Hegel raised the state to the level of the all-informing principle that shapes and molds the character of human beings as citizens and subjects. In contrast, democracy begins with the free, rational human being who creates the state according to his/her own projected image.

It is remarkable that the young Marx entertained thoughts of one analogy after the other in the *Critique*, probably assuming that a figure of speech in which one thing is likened to another may imply the existence of proof. For example, what does it mean that "democracy is the Old Testament of all other forms of state?"[54] What does this analogy signify in terms of individual liberty in the context of a historical reality? How does it contribute to our understanding of democracy? And, finally, is there a "gospel of democracy" based on some notions from the Old Testament?

Marx is even less careful when he declares that "in some respects democracy is related to all other forms of state, as Christianity is related to all other religions"[55]—a comforting but hardly convincing belief in the superiority of Christianity, which the young Marx shared with Hegel.

To anyone who has learned to look at Marx and his doctrine with critical eyes, it is obvious that in his "treatment" of democracy in the *Critique*, Marx played with abstractions, analogies, categories, symbols, and everything except content. Moreover, a meticulous reading of the *Critique* shows that Marx never dealt with real and concrete issues of democracy, such as the right to opposition and the commitment to a democratic leadership accountable to the people. It seems that scholars who accept with enthusiastic praise the writings of the young Marx are overlooking Engels's embarassing remark in the 1880s that Marx's juvenilia "were as unimportant as Marx's youthful poetry and unreadable in their semi-Hegelian language."[56]

When Marx assumed the job of editor of the *Neue Rheinische Zei-*

tung in 1848, he reported on the proceedings of the elected Frankfurt Assembly with a sense of growing contempt for democracy in general and for the parliamentary system in particular. As a matter of fact, gradualism, political moderation, and the "so-called rights of man"[57] earned Marx's disdain, despite his acquittal by a bourgeois jury on a charge of sedition. From that point on, Marx grew increasingly scornful of anything democratic.

Curiously, some sympathetic critics of Marx claim that Benedict Spinoza exerted a great influence on the young Marx while he was working on the rough draft of the *Critique*. As evidence, they point to one of Marx's notebooks, which is preserved in the International Institute of Social History in Amsterdam, dating from 1841–1842, when he was a student in Berlin. This notebook contains one hundred and sixty excerpts from Spinoza's *Tractatus Theologico-Politicus* without a single personal comment or criticism.[58]

It is possible that the young Marx borrowed some ideas on democracy from Spinoza, but he certainly did not adapt Spinoza's simple, clear-cut, and concise style of expression. It seems that the young Marx was much more influenced by Hegel's philosophy and terminology, since the *Critique* offers many examples in which practical issues of political theory are treated in abstract terms that stand as a substitute for plain common sense. It is not that Marx's metaphorical sentences verge, at times, on artificiality; it is simply that, on the whole, Spinoza's straightforward, declarative statements are much more crisp, austere and to the point. Thus Spinoza states:

> This corporate right, which is defined by the power of the people, is generally called sovereignty, and is entirely vested in those who by common consent manage the affairs of the state, i.e., who make, interpret, and repeal laws, fortify cities, make decisions about war and peace, and so on. If such functions belong to a general assembly of the people, then the state is called a democracy.[59]

The reading of this passage did not restrain the more mature Marx from speaking contemptuously of the "democratic rabble" that brings "daily the pestiferous affluvia of the democratic sinkhole."[60] In contrast, however, regardless of their contempt for democracy, Marx and Engels appropriated the term "democracy" for the fledgling Communist movement, using words such as "proletariat," "democracy," and "the people" interchangeably, as if they conveyed the same meaning. In fact, as early as 1843, Engels argued that "the industrial proletariat has become the vanguard of all modern democracy, and that the communists for the time being . . . take the field as democrats."[61] This is a clever propagandistic ploy utilized to identify democracy—in a distorted sense, of course—with Communism and the proletariat (which Marx raised to a divine status); this tactic was also used successfully by Lenin and his heirs many years later. And this stratagem is also featured in the *Communist Manifesto*: "The first step in the revolution by the working class is to raise the proletariat to the position of the ruling class, to win the battle of democracy."[62]

Not surprisingly, Marx fails to explain what it really means "to win the battle for democracy" (*Die Erkämpfung der Demokratie*) or what the theoretical and practical ramifications of the concept "democracy" are in the *Manifesto*. Reading his other works, it becomes immediately evident that, for Marx, democracy is without meaning unless one is referring to the class that is actually in power. It is quite clear that the mature Marx showed little concern for the workings of a democratic pluralist system. No form of reflection or inference can create this knowledge and commitment if one is wholeheartedly and impatiently dedicated to violent change, representing a negation of the democratic pluralist system in which elected government and its institutions normally provide mechanisms for the expression of common interests among the political groups—mechanisms that, above all, make possible a *peaceful* conciliation and compromise of their differing interests.

As soon as we look more closely into the presuppositions of the Marxian doctrine, we realize that Marx never answers questions such as: Is proletarian democracy representative of the community? How will proletarian democracy strive for the common good? Will the authority to rule derive from the community? And finally, how is proletarian democracy compatible with democratic institutions? Marx leaves these realistic questions unanswered because, in his utopian vision, the concept of democracy becomes superfluous to the political framework of the state withering away—a sheer phantasm, to say the least.

In 1850, with the barricades, the street fighting, and the revolutionary events of 1848 still fresh in mind, Marx prepared the *Address of the Central Committee to the Communist League*.[63] In this secret document, Marx predicted that the democratic petit bourgeoisie would be successful in overthrowing the reigning monarchy in Germany. However, Marx, as a theorist of the class struggle, not only outlined the strategy and tactics of the Communist League but also sharply attacked the democrats, condemning democracy regardless of how progressive or reformist a democratic government might be.

Convinced that parliamentary democracy in a bourgeois state was the most complete form of "alien politics," to be viewed as a prelude to the revolutionary eradication of this symptom of alienation, Marx declared in a letter written on August 2, 1851: "The whole local democratic vermin deposits its manure in the ditch there, but no seeds or fruits, making the weeds flourish luxuriantly."[64] A few years later, in a comment in the weekly *Hermann* published in London, Marx states in less vitriolic terms: "Anything more wretched has never been published, and we can only congratulate ourselves that in the ten-year exile of our democratic friends their hollowness has never been more exposed."[65]

But the most obvious lack of appreciation of democratic principles, in the juridical and symbolic sense emerged in Marx's *Critique of the Gotha Program*.[66] The Gotha Program sealed the affiliation of the socialist Eisenach faction—close to Marx and Engels—with the Lassallean Party, thereby marking the formation of a single, united German Social Democratic Party in 1875. Marx, deeply displeased with the spirit of compromise in the joint Gotha Program, was particularly angered by the "misguided" directives calling for the organization of state-aided workers' cooperatives in lieu of a violent, revolutionary transformation of society. Written in the form of marginal notes, the *Critique of the Gotha Program* expressed Marx's beliefs regarding the establishment of a militant socialist party and how it should forge its political and revolutionary program. But above all, Marx conveyed his utter contempt for the "old democratic litany familiar to all: universal suffrage, direct legislation, popular rights, a people's militia, etc."[67] As H. Stuart Hughes, the author of the authoritative study *Consciousness and Society*, observes, "This antithesis between the Marx of wrath and the Marx of sweet reason had, of course, always existed."[68]

And how far sweet reason could take the young Marx—when he still entertained ideas of being useful to *humanity* at large—is evident in the following statements, dating back to 1843. Protesting against the restrictions of a rigid dogmatism, Marx declares: "We do not confront the world in a doctrinaire way with a new principle: Here is the truth, kneel down before it! We develop new principles for the world out of the world's own principles."[69]

But this task is possible only if man is part of a free, democratic community, and accordingly, the young Marx states:

> The self-respect (*Selbstgefühl*) of man, his freedom, must still be awakened in the breasts of these men. Only this feeling of self-respect, which disappeared with the Greeks from the world and into the blue haze of

the heavens with the Christians, can make out of society once more a community of men in pursuit of their highest end, the *democratic state*.[70]

This ringing endorsement of a democratic state, however, dating back to his youthful days, apparently rested on insecure foundations. In the years of his embittered exile, Marx's harsh and hostile pronouncements are aimed at so-called human rights and universal suffrage as well as at a host of democratic institutions and values —pronouncements that shatter the whole substance and validity of the musings of a young man enchanted by democratic ideas.

Only two years before his death, unhappy with the institutionalization of democratic procedures within the German Social Democratic movement, Marx declared:

> I regard all workers' congresses and socialist congresses, insofar as they are not directly related to the conditions existing in this or that particular nation, as not merely useless but actually harmful. They will always fade away in innumerable, stale, general banalities.[71]

And to avoid any doctrinal confusion, Marx explains what he means by "conditions existing in this or that particular nation" in the context of the same letter:

> The ever growing fury into which the masses are lashed by the old ghostly governments, while at the same time the positive development of the means of production advances with gigantic strides—all this is sufficient guarantee that the moment a real proletarian revolution breaks out—the conditions of its immediately next *modus operandi* [i.e., the dictatorship of the proletariat] will be in existence.[72]

Thus it is impossible to evaluate Marx's views on democracy objectively without taking into consideration this duality of impulses in the thought of the young Marx and the revolutionary posture of the more mature Marx. This duality of impulses must be sharply distinguished and separated in terms of its contradictory and mutually exclusive qualities, stripped of any intellectual and logical kinship. Once we establish this fact, it becomes quite clear that despite the attempts of some scholars to single out the views on democracy that Marx held in his youth, these views cannot be attributed to Marx as if held throughout his lifetime. The effort to portray Marx as a humanist and a lifelong democrat is a willful misrepresentation of existing evidence, accessible to anyone who is willing to study the collected works of Marx—preferably in their original form—including his numerous letters written to friends and foes, which reveal most clearly the political and philosophical convictions of the Father of Communism.

The refusal to draw a demarcation line between the young and the mature Marx, and the persistent claim that the whole of Marx forms a clear and coherent unity only if it is viewed from the perspective of his early writings, is at its worst when it implies that generations of Marxists, Lenin included, founded a revolutionary movement and propagated their ideas with defective or incomplete understanding of the "true" Marx, having no access to the *Economic and Philosophical Manuscripts of 1844*, which did not see the light of day before their publication in 1932.

Almost one hundred and fifty years ago, Heinrich Heine, in his romantic interpretation of the French Revolution, made the comment that Maximilien Robespierre was merely the hand of Jean-Jacques Rousseau.[73] To paraphrase Heine, if Robespierre was merely Rousseau's hand, and if men of action are nothing but unconscious instruments of men of thought, then Lenin was the hand of Karl Marx—the hand that literally drew from the womb of time the body whose soul Marx had created.

This transposition of the poet's observation displays in more than a metaphoric sense all its dimension of pure meaning. The historical core of this insight becomes strikingly evident as soon as we compare the major aspects of the relationship between Marx and Lenin. Both men were dedicated to disseminating among the working masses the consciousness of their destiny, thus expediting their preparedness for the forthcoming revolutionary tasks. Accordingly, Marx believed that, in the long run, the working class would acquire on its own a revolutionary consciousness and organization. However, Lenin did not share this confidence—hence, his distrust of the working class and his coldly calculated belief in a new type of party, headed by intellectuals turned into professional revolutionaries and aggrandized as the vanguard of the working class.

Furthermore, Marx, as well as Lenin, considered the class struggle more than a struggle for social reform. In their view, the class conflicts represented a long-range process leading to a social revolution, with the rise to power of the working class—supposedly a class capable of bringing about a total reorganization of society. Both men shared the view that

> the Communists . . . are on the one hand, practically, the most advanced and resolute section of the working-class parties of every country, that section which pushes forward all others; on the other hand, theoretically, they have over the great mass of the proletariat the advantage of clearly understanding the line of march, the conditions, and the ultimate general results of the proletarian movement.[74]

It was this idea, originated by Marx, that inspired Lenin's conception of a highly disciplined organization of "professional revolutionaries," the Bolsheviks. And finally, both men used—or rather misused freely—the democratic label in the name of expediency. In reality, democracy, in their view, represented a mode of expression of bourgeois society's ineradicable antagonisms. In 1903, before the split in the Russian Social Democratic Party, Lenin stated:

> The bourgeois democrat (and the modern opportunist Socialist who walks in his footsteps) imagines that democracy eliminates the class struggle; and that is why he presents all his political demands in an abstract, sweeping, "unqualified" way from the standpoint of the interests of the "whole people'" or even from that of an eternal and absolute moral principle. The Social-Democrat will always and everywhere ruthlessly expose this bourgeois illusion.[75]

Inspired by an inextinguishable hatred of the czarist regime, Lenin, in his early twenties, reinforced this frame of mind, not only pursuing underground revolutionary activity but also acquiring a "wonderful knowledge of Marx, thus achieving an outstanding position as a Marxist able to expound the cause in terms that the ordinary reader and listener could understand."[76] It is not surprising, therefore, that as early as 1899, when Lenin was twenty-nine years old—he declared: "We do not regard Marx's theory as something completed and inviolable; on the contrary, we are convinced that it has only laid the foundation stone of the science which socialists *must* develop in all directions if they wish to keep pace with life."[77]

To be sure, Lenin's contributions to revolutionary strategy, to Marxist economics and sociology, are beyond dispute. Still, ideas expressed in his articles, books, and pamphlets echo in many respects Marx's contempt for the "old democratic litany familiar to all."[78] Equally disdainful of democratic values, and despite his frequent sojourns to the West, Lenin states in his pamphlet *The Tasks of the Russian Social-*

Democrats (1902): "The petty bourgeoisie is two-faced by its very nature, and while it gravitates, on the one hand, towards the proletariat and democracy, on the other, it gravitates towards the reactionary classes, (and) tries to hold up the march of history."[79]

A few years later, in his attempt to distinguish attitudes of working-class democrats from attitudes of bourgeois democrats, Lenin states: "History has . . . afforded us hundreds of instances in which bourgeois democrats came forward with slogans demanding, not only full liberty, but also equality, with socialist slogans—without thereby ceasing to be bourgeois democrats—and thus 'befogged' the minds of the proletariat all the more."[80]

On the eve of the October Revolution, Lenin's invectives against democracy and the parliamentary system reached new heights. In his *State and Revolution*—a work expounding the Marxist theory of the state and the tasks of the proletariat in the revolution—Lenin calls for the abolition of "the venal and rotten parliamentarism of bourgeois society institutions in which freedom of opinion and discussion . . . degenerate into a deception. . . . We can and must imagine democracy without parliamentarism."[81] But Lenin did not stop with his cynical contempt for democratic parliamentarism. Within days after the seizure of power by the Bolsheviks, Lenin ordered the closure of all newspapers, declaring that

> we Bolsheviki have always said that when we reached a position of power we could close the bourgeois press. To tolerate the bourgeois newspapers would mean to cease being a Socialist. When one makes a Revolution one cannot mark time; one must always go forward—or go back. He who now talks about the "freedom of the Press" goes backward, and halts our headlong course toward Socialism.[82]

The following is a quotation from a democratic publication of November 28, 1917, a few days before its forced closing:

> We are under the threat of a counterrevolution. . . . It is not true. . . . The counterrevolution has already taken place. What are the goals of this counterrevolution? The suppression of civil liberties; the dissolution of all political parties; the dispersal of freely elected representatives of the people, and the incarceration or deportation of the most prominent leaders of the revolutionary movement.[83]

An air of exultant lawlessness reigned at the end of the crucial year 1917. As Reinhard Bendix observed, "Where norms can be changed at a moment's notice, the rule of law is destroyed."[84] On December

20, 1917, on Lenin's orders, the new Soviet government established the All-Russian Commission for Suppression of Counter-Revolution, Sabotage, and Speculation, the first Communist secret police, known as the CHEKA. This notorious instrument of Bolshevik policies functioned as a special organ of the Russian Communist Party, directly under Lenin's control.[85] With the restoration of the death penalty in February, 1918, the CHEKA started its work of exterminating all political rivals. The Kadet Party was outlawed and orders were issued for the arrest of Mensheviks and Social Revolutionaries—people "who had fought just as hard as the Bolsheviks for socialism, but not socialism of this kind, socialism imposed by terror."[86] About four years later, apparently dissatisfied with the "progress" in exterminating political opponents, Lenin turned over this task to Stalin in a now-famous letter written on July 17, 1922, and published in *The New York Times* on June 15, 1992:

Comrade Stalin!
On the matter of deporting Mensheviks, National Socialists, Kadets, etc. from Russia, I would like to ask a few questions, since this operation, which started before my leave, still has not been completed.
Has the decision been made to "eradicate" all the NS's? [National Socialists] Peshkonov, Myakotin, Gornfeld, Petrishchev, et al.?
As far as I am concerned, deport them all. (They are) more harmful than any SR (Socialist Revolutionary)—because (they are) more clever.
Also A. N. Potresov, Izgoyev and all the "Ekonomist" contributors (Ozerov and many, many others). The Mensheviks, Rozanov (a physician, cunning), Vigdorchik, (Migulov or something like that), Liubov Nikolayevna Radchenko and her young daughter (rumor has it they're the vilest enemies of Bolshevism), N. A. Rozhkov (he has to be deported; incorrigible); S. A. Frank (author of "Metodologia"). The commission supervised by Mantsev, Messing et al. should present lists and several hundred such ladies and gentlemen must be deported without mercy. Let's purge Russia for a long while!
This must be done at once. Before the end of the SRs' trial, no later. Arrest a few hundred and without a declaration of motives—get out, ladies and gentlemen!

With a communist greeting
LENIN

In a similar approach, on August 9, 1918, Lenin, faced with peasant insurrections in the Penza province, urged the Penza Executive Committee to carry out "ruthless mass terror against the kulaks, priests, and White Guards," exhorting the Penza Committee to "confine all suspicious elements in a concentration camp outside the city."[87] After this instrument of terror was widely deployed in the fledgling Soviet state, the method of repression was legalized by a decree of the *Sovnarkom* (Council of People's Commissars), which stated: "It is necessary to protect the Soviet Republic from class enemies by isolating them in concentration camps."[88]

Thus, during the first months after the October Revolution, a new state was born—a totalitarian state. Under these circumstances, "democracy"—in terms of an accountable executive, an uncoerced legislature, and an independent judiciary—had no place in the operational code of the Bolsheviks. Nevertheless, as the leader of a disciplined, tightly knit revolutionary party, quite distinct from the working class by virtue of its organization, Lenin was subjected to frequent criticism for suppressing party democracy. Lenin defended himself with the claim that Bolshevism implies the establishment of authority that is then translated into the subordination of lower party bodies to the central leadership of the Party.

However, in totalitarian politics, words suffer from gradual distortion and are, at times, subject to complete inversions of their original meanings. This type of perversion is encountered in the so-called democratic centralism—a term coined by Lenin and conceived to justify the subordination of the lower party bodies to the central leadership of the Party. It is obvious that "democratic centralism" represented a fusion of two irreconcilable factors, which in their combination highlighted one of the most prominent Communist precepts, a precept "which serve[d] only to conceal a reality of centralism—that is of autocracy, dictatorship, or totalitarianism."[89] Following in Lenin's footsteps, Soviet theoreticians elevated this precept to a system of thought and practice that in reality, amounted to a theory of domination and intolerance, reflected in the CPSU's (Communist Party of the Soviet Union) statutes of 1934 with an emphasis on its major clause: "The decisions of higher bodies are absolutely binding on lower bodies and on party members."[90] And of course, *absolutely* binding decisions refer to thinking as well as behavior.

If the 1936 Stalin Constitution did not include democratic centralism in its official version, the Brezhnev Constitution, adopted on October 7, 1977, extended this precept, imposing "Leninist norms" on the neo-Stalinist structure of the entire state, proclaiming proudly that "the Soviet state is organized and functions on the principle of democratic centralism" (Article 3).[91] Accordingly, Soviet theoreticians defined democratic centralism as follows: "The clearest reflection of the scientific, planned and democratic character of social management is the principle of democratic centralism—the basic principle of organization and government in a socialist society."[92]

Needless to say, this principle was defined for Soviet citizens in a way the party had chosen to define it, and consequently, it did not begin to reflect the strains and shifts in the political practices of the Bolsheviks[93]—practices that foreclosed any frank criticism of party policies and led to the violent suppression of the opposition in the bloody purges and to a passionate quest for unanimity and unity of action.

Hailing the Brezhnev Constitution as "a historical landmark in the development of Soviet society,"[94] Marxist-Leninist writers extolled the broad rights granted to the Soviet people—rights that guaranteed "freedom of speech," of the press, and of assembly, meetings, street processions and demonstrations."[95] A careful reading of Article 50 of the constitution shows clearly that all these rights were indeed guaranteed by law. However, these same rights were virtually invalidated by a qualifying clause, formulated in the opening sentence of Article 50, which distinctly states that these laws were granted only "in accordance with the interests of the people and in order to strengthen and develop the socialist system."[96] It is obvious that this qualifying clause made a mockery of these so-called rights, since in the neo-Stalinist environment only the Soviet government or the KGB decided what the real interests of the people were. Taking advantage of this qualifying clause, Soviet security organs—in the name of socialist legality—persecuted, incarcerated, and tortured Soviet citizens whose political thinking did not conform to the official canons of Marxist-Leninist ideology. The constitutional expert S. E. Finer offered in 1979 the following comment on the actual meaning of "socialist legality":

> The recent efforts at revising the Civil and Criminal Codes, culminating in the new Brezhnev Constitution itself, are attempts to give the fundamentally illiberal and despotic behavior of the state's authorities the veneer of "socialist legality." In practice such "socialist legality" is often a sophisticated and perverse legalism.[97]

In other words, the resurgence of dictatorial methods and the suppression of any democratic tendencies in the totalitarian-bureaucratic environment of the neo-Stalinist state were undertaken in the name of "socialist legality" (a subject matter rarely explored by mainline Sovietologists) and hailed as a judicial doctrine in Orwellian language. In reality, this judicial doctrine was hardly concerned with the rights of the individual citizens, being much more preoccupied with fulfilling the "historic tasks" of the Party: enforcing "state discipline" and protecting "socialist" property.

However, the bureaucratic-totalitarian potential was not limited to the failure to provide juridical and political freedoms. Regardless of the empty and ritualistic character of Soviet political life, polluted with the doctrinaire legacy of Marx, Engels, Lenin, and Stalin, the Soviet government also sought to legitimize its total rule by attempting to control and condition every person's mind and to confine citizens' outlook to a narrow, totalitarian concept of the world.

Notes

1. Victor Zaslavsky, *The Neo-Stalinist State* (Armonk, New York: M. E. Sharpe, 1982), 131.

2. Wherever he or she turned, the Soviet citizen was exposed to "huge political slogans hung from the rooftops, draped from bridges and hotel balconies or fixed in a firmament of lights in downtown squares: 'Lenin is Our Banner,' 'The Party and the People are United,' 'Communism Will Win,' 'Lift High the Banner of Proletarian Internationalism,' 'Glory to the Soviet People, Builders of Communism,' or simply 'Glory to Work.'" Hedrick Smith, *The Russians* (New York: Quadrangle, The New York Times Book Co., 1976), 284.

3. V. G. Afanasyev, N. V. Chernogolovkin, et al., eds., *Soviet Democracy in the Period of Developed Socialism* (Moscow: Progress Publishers, 1979), 53.

4. Timothy W. Luke, "Civil Religion and Secularization: Ideological Revitalization in Post-revolutionary Communist Systems," *Sociological Forum* 2, no. 1 (1987): 111 and 117. Emphasis added.

5. N. Chalyapin, "On the Verge of a Great Tragedy," *Argumenty i Fakty* no. 39 (Moscow, 1989): 1–2.

6. Stephen F. Cohen, *Rethinking the Soviet Experience* (New York and Oxford: Oxford University Press, 1985), 146. A similar argument is offered by Jerry F. Hough in *The Soviet Union and Social Science Theory* (Cambridge: Harvard University Press, 1977), 3. Emphasis added.

7. David Lane, *The Soviet Economy and Society* (New York: New York University Press, 1985), xii.

8. Ibid., 96–97.

9. Ibid.

10. Cited in Stephen R. Burant, "The Influence of Russian Tradition on the Political Style of the Soviet Elite," *Political Science Quarterly* (Summer 1987): 274.

11. After reading a number of biographies of Lenin, Trotsky, and Stalin—in particular Dmitri Volkogonov's *Stalin: Triumph and Tragedy* (New York: Grove Weidenfeld, 1991) and *Trotsky* (Moscow: Novosti, 1992)—it is

obvious that revolutionary leaders were primarily motivated by a resolve to seize and entrench themselves in power, no matter what the cost.

12. Cited in Leszek Kolakowski, *The Alienation of Reason* (New York: Doubleday Anchor Books, 1969), 198.

13. John Plamenatz, *German Marxism and Russian Communism* (London: Longmans, Green and Co., 1954), 56.

14. Ibid., 159. Emphasis added.

15. Ibid., 159–60.

16. David W. Lovell, *From Marx to Lenin* (New York and Cambridge: Cambridge University Press, 1984), 197.

17. A. Amalrik, "Russia and the Perplexing Prospects of Liberty," in *Eurocommunism, Its Roots and Future in Italy and Elsewhere*, ed. G. Urban (London: Temple Smith, 1978), 252.

18. D. J. Manning and T. J. Robinson, *The Place of Ideology in Political Life* (London: Croom Helm Ltd., 1985), 47.

19. Cited in Louis Fischer, *The Life of Lenin* (New York: Harper & Row Publishers, 1964), 150.

20. Sir John Maynard, *Russia in Flux* (New York: The Macmillan Co., 1948), 252.

21. A slightly altered version of this section appeared as Sigmund Krancberg, "Karl Marx and Democracy," *Studies in Soviet Thought* 24 (1985): 23–35, © 1985 by D. Reidel Publishing Company; reprinted by permission of Kluwer Academic Publishers.

22. Arthur C. Danto, *Nietzsche as Philosopher* (New York: Macmillan Co., 1965), 67.

23. *Writings of the Young Marx on Philosophy and Society*, ed. and trans. Loyd D. Easton and Kurt H. Guddat (Garden City, N.Y.: Doubleday & Co., 1967), 151–202; henceforth referred to as *Writings*. (The Easton Guddat translation of the *Kritik des Hegelschen Staatsrechts* is by far more faithful to the original text in Karl Marx, Friedrich Engels, *Werke*, Band 1 [Berlin: Dietz Verlag, 1961].)

24. Sidney Hook, *Revolution, Reform, and Social Justice* (New York: New York University Press, 1975), 1.

25. Karl Marx, *Critique of Hegel's Philosophy of Right*, ed. Joseph O'Malley (New York and Cambridge: Cambridge University Press, 1970), Editor's Introduction, xv, henceforth referred to as the *Critique*.

26. Jon Elster, *Making Sense of Marx* (New York and Cambridge: Cambridge University Press, 1985), 446.

27. Robert C. Tucker, ed., *The Marx-Engels Reader*, 2d edition (New York: W. W. Norton & Co., 1978), 545, henceforth referred to as *Reader*.

28. Maximilien Rubel, "Notes on Marx's Conception of Democracy," *New Politics* 1 (1962): 79–80.

29. Ibid., 79.

30. Robert Heilbroner, *Marxism: For or Against* (New York: W. W. Norton & Co., 1980), 46.

31. Ernst Topitsch, "How Enlightened is Dialectical Reason," *Encounter* (May, 1982): 46.

32. The dialectical focus on "contradictions," however, might explain how the collapse of the Soviet system followed the apparently most stable and accepted period of Soviet rule. American Sovietology, blind to the underlying tensions in Soviet life, simply extrapolated then-current trends into the indefinite future.

33. As Sidney Hook observed: "Since the traditional formulation of this method is burdened with many misleading and mistaken conceptions, it would be more conducive to clear thinking if the phrase were dropped." *Dialectical Materialism and Scientific Method* (Manchester, England: The Committee on Science and Freedom, 1954), 27.

34. Rubel, "Notes," 79.

35. Adam Schaff, *Marxism and the Human Individual*, with an introduction by Erich Fromm (New York: McGraw Hill, 1970), x.

36. David L. Prychitko, *Marxism and Workers' Self-Management* (Westport, Conn.: Greenwood Press, 1991), xiii.

37. Ibid. Emphasis added.

38. Leszek Kolakowski, "Three Motifs in Marxism," in *Kontinent 2* (New York: Anchor Books, 1977), 167.

39. Sidney Hook, *Marx and the Marxists: The Ambiguous Legacy* (Princeton, N.J.: D. Van Nostrand Co., 1955), 85.

40. Hook, *Revolution, Reform, and Social Justice*, 71.

41. Ibid., 71–72.

42. See Edward Hallet Carr, *Karl Marx: A Study in Fanaticism* (London: J. M. Dent, 1934).

43. Karl Marx, *Economic and Philosophical Manuscripts of 1844* (New York: International Publishers, 1964).

44. *Writings*, 173.

45. Ibid.

46. *Hegel's Science of Logic*, trans. A. V. Miller (New York: Humanities Press, 1969), 528–29.

47. *Writings*, 173.

48. *Hegel's Philosophy of Right*, trans. T. M. Knox (New York: Oxford Press, 1952), 288.

49. Ibid., 279.

50. Ibid., 288.

51. Ibid., 279.

52. Isaiah Berlin, *Karl Marx* (New York and London: Oxford University Press, 1963), 10.

53. *Writings*, 173.

54. Ibid., 174.

55. Ibid.

56. Ibid., 2.

57. Cited in Henri Lefebvre, *The Sociology of Marx* (New York: Pantheon Books, 1968), 132.

58. Rubel, "Notes," 81.

59. Benedict de Spinoza, *The Political Works* (New York and London: Oxford University Press, 1958), 278–79.

60. *The Letters of Karl Marx*, trans. Saul K. Padover (Englewood Cliffs, N.J.: Prentice Hall, 1979), 73. Henceforth referred to as *Letters*.
61. Cited in Lovell, *From Marx to Lenin*, 34.
62. *Reader*, 490.
63. Ibid., 501.
64. *Letters*, 72.
65. Ibid., 132.
66. *Reader*, 525–41.
67. Ibid., 538.
68. H. Stuart Hughes, *Consciousness and Society* (New York: Vintage Books, 1958), 71.
69. *Letters*, 32.
70. Cited in Hook, *Revolution, Reform, and Social Justice*, 83–84. Emphasis added.
71. Cited in Gavin Kitching, *Karl Marx and the Philosophy of Praxis* (London: Routledge, 1988), 130.
72. Ibid.
73. Heinrich Heine, *Religion and Philosophy in Germany* (Boston: Beacon Press, 1959), 106.
74. *Reader*, 484.
75. V. I. Lenin, *Selected Works,* vol. 2 (New York: International Publishers, 1943), 324.
76. Ronald W. Clark, *Lenin* (New York: Harper and Row Publishers, 1988), 33. Clark cites this observation based on N. K. Krupskaya's memoirs.
77. V. I. Lenin, *Collected Works*, vol. 4 (Moscow: Progress Publishers, 1960), 211–12.
78. *Reader*, 538.
79. V. I. Lenin, *Collected Works*, vol. 2 (Moscow: Foreign Languages Publishing House, 1960), 335.
80. Ibid., vol. 8, 75.
81. V. I. Lenin, *Selected Works*, vol. 2 (New York: International Publishers, 1967), 302.
82. John Reed, *Ten Days That Shook the World* (New York: Vintage Books, 1960), 356.
83. *Novaya Riech* (New Discourse), (November 28, 1917); cited in *Ogoniok* (Small Light), no. 45 (1991): 2.
84. Cited in A. J. Polan, *Lenin and the End of Politics* (Berkeley: University of California Press, 1984), 113.
85. Mikhail Heller and Alexander Nekrich, *Utopia in Power* (New York: Summit Books, 1985), 65. Henceforth referred to as *Utopia in Power*.
86. Alan Moorehead, *The Russian Revolution* (New York: Harper & Brothers, 1985), 262.
87. *Utopia in Power*, 66.
88. Ibid.
89. Michael Waller, *Democratic Centralism: A Historical Commentary* (Manchester: Manchester University, 1981), 5.

90. Cited in Ronald Tiersky, *Ordinary Stalinism* (Boston: George Allen & Unwin, Boston, 1955), 44.

91. Boris Toporkin, *The New Constitution of the USSR* (Moscow: Progress Publishers, 1980), 237. Henceforth referred to as *The New Constitution*.

92. *Soviet Democracy in the Period of Developed Socialism*, 137.

93. For example: the arrest of Beria, the 1964 coup or the failed 1991 coup—all important evidence regarding the real meaning of democratic centralism.

94. *Soviet Democracy*, 6.

95. *The New Constitution*, 254. (Article 50 of the Brezhnev Constitution is almost identical with Article 125 of Stalin's Constitution of 1936.)

96. Ibid.

97. Cited in Tiersky, *Ordinary Stalinism*, 260.

4

Controlling Individual Development and Behavior

> The Russian is a bad worker compared with people in advanced countries. The task that the Soviet government must set the people in all its scope is—learn to work . . . working to raise the productivity of labor (during) the transition period from capitalism to socialism . . . require(s) the use of compulsion, so that the slogan of the dictatorship of the proletariat shall not be desecrated by the practice of a lily-livered proletarian government.
>
> V. I. Lenin (April, 1918)[1]

Prefatory Note

Since the establishment of the Soviet state, the doctrines of Marxism-Leninism exerted an enormous influence in the shaping and conditioning of Soviet thought.[2] Following the tenets of Marxism-Leninism formulated in the concepts of dialectical and historical materialism, and treating these doctrines with a curious respect—as if no one could have any objections—Soviet philosophers loyally submitted to the ideological dictates of the Communist Party, hardly aware that the more elaborate and demanding the ideological commitment, the less relevant the philosopher's point of view.

To discourage any deviations from its guidelines, the Communist Party periodically reasserted its commanding role over the essence and structure of philosophical endeavor and issued veiled warnings about instances of "scholastic theorizing with quite a few philosophers seeking to prove what has already been proven."[3] Formless and unpredictable, the warnings were vague in character and devoid of any explanation regarding the substance of these potential "errors." Still, there was something distinctly schizophrenic in such attempts to tighten the ideological controls while simultaneously and strongly recommending that recent "developments in society's political life [had to] be analyzed more profoundly and with greater courage."[4] Regardless of the schizophrenic quality of these exhortations, under the authoritative patronage of the Communist Party, courage and a profound, free inquiry into matters of fact and truth were not the governing standards of Soviet philosophy—a philosophy that was never separated from Marxist-Leninist ideology.

In its determination to exert a controlling influence over all aspects of the moral upbringing of the "new Soviet man," the party's undisputed authority was particularly evident in the field of Soviet theoretical ethics. That is, Soviet ethical culture was heavily infused with Marxist-Leninist precepts, which were handled as high ideals of human conduct to be realized in the process of a "necessary, natural, and historically long period in the form of the Communist system."[5] Only the Communist Party set the general tone and content in matters of ethical substance concerning the central image of man, while Soviet ethicists, in deference to their ideological elders, simply filled in the details necessary to the larger framework provided by the party. To be sure, Soviet moral philosophers were involved in protracted disputes regarding minor, isolated issues and, as a matter of habit, tended to support their views either with references to a resolution adapted at the last Party Congress or with outworn citations from the "classics" of Marxism-Leninism—as if only the party or the "classics" could have furnished a clearly ordered picture of the moral universe.

Richard T. De George, the author of a magisterial study on Soviet ethics,[6] has observed that "the basis of morality has never been discussed or debated in Soviet ethical literature but merely stated and generally accepted. . . . From the beginning, however, Soviet ethics were stillborn, for it lacked philosophical life."[7]

After Stalin's death, Soviet philosophy experienced an upsurge of interest in problems of formal ethical theory. There was an intense search for more precise definitions of morality, long considered an element of social consciousness and regarded in Marxist-Leninist terms as part of the ideological superstructure. This Marxist connection between social consciousness and the economic base restricted the inquiry into morality to three constitutive categories of social being: moral consciousness, moral action, and moral relations. Some Soviet philosophers identified morality with moral action and moral consciousness—two basic categories reflecting "norms of human behavior objectively taking shape in society in such concepts as 'the good,' 'honesty,' 'conscience,' 'justice,' etc., which have an evaluative character."[8] Other philosophers considered "moral relations" the most important component of morality, since moral relations exist outside consciousness and are manifestations of the day-to-day practical relations among people.[9] Excluding from these discussions such vital ingredients of moral behavior as the maximization of the good, moral competence, empathy, reciprocity, and moral responsibility (Soviet philosophers treated moral responsibility under the rubric of "social responsibility"), other Soviet philosophers chose all three categories—moral consciousness, moral action, and moral relations—as the constitutive elements of morality.

Lively polemics on the topic of ethics as a "philosophical science," covering a broad spectrum of views on the relation between ethics and morality, were common in Soviet ethical literature. A group of Soviet philosophers argued that ethics is related to the class of philosophical sciences and, ipso facto, is a form of consciousness and therefore forms a part of humanity's worldview.[10] The editors of the *Dictionary of Philosophy*[11] disagreed with this dual characterization of ethics and morality. According to M. Rosenthal and P. Yudin,

> Ethics, the science of morals, includes normative ethics and the theory of morals. Ethics . . . elaborates a moral code of behavior, showing what is worth striving for, what behavior is good and what gives meaning to life. The theory of morals deals with the essence of morality, its origin and development, the laws which determine standards and their historical character.[12]

Of course, they added, it was Marx and Engels who proved that morality is determined by the economic and social system of society, and consequently, morality is a historical product. In the final analysis, ethics is not a derivative of the sum total of moral knowledge; ethics and morals are in constant interaction and are inseparable.[13] However, the editors of the *Dictionary of Philosophy* were unable to affirm, from the historical perspective, that ethical principles and moral consciousness have a certain characteristic autonomy of their own.[14]

With the mode of Soviet thought totally subordinate to party ideology, discussions on ethics displayed a remarkable tendency to classify and generalize the concepts of "Communist morality," with absolutely no attempt to analyze critically sensitive political and philosophical issues. Commenting on moral concepts and the structure of morality and reflecting, no doubt, the tension between theoretical ethics and ideology, a leading Soviet philosopher, L. M. Arxange'lskij, neatly summarized the ongoing discussions in Soviet ethical literature as a number of problems that simply remained poorly worked out.[15]

Totally ignoring the questions raised by ethical theoreticians as moot or irrelevant, the Communist Party of the Soviet Union, without prior notice or public discussion, adopted in 1961 at its Twenty-second Congress a new Party Programme which incorporated a moral code for the "builder" of communism.

The programme announced to the world that, by 1980, a Communist society would be built in the USSR.[16] Stressing the importance of moral principles in the course of this transition to communism, the party defined the rules of behavior in the moral code as "fundamental norms of human morality which the masses of the people evolved in the course of millennia as they fought against vice and social oppression."[17] Declaring that these elementary standards of morality and justice were to be considered as inviolable rules for relations between both individuals and peoples, the party proclaimed that the *Moral Code of the Builder of Communism* should comprise the following principles:

   1. Devotion to the Communist cause; love of the socialist motherland and of the other socialist countries.
   2. Conscientious labor for the good of society—he who does not work, neither shall he eat.
   3. Concern on the part of everyone for the preservation and growth of public wealth.
   4. A high sense of public duty; intolerance of actions harmful to the public interest.
   5. Collectivism and comradely mutual assistance; one for all and all for one.
   6. Humane relations and mutual respect between individuals—man to man is a friend, comrade, and brother.
   7. Honesty and truthfulness, moral purity, modesty, and unpretentiousness in social and private life.
   8. Mutual respect in the family and concern for the upbringing of children.
   9. An uncompromising attitude to injustice, parasitism, dishonesty, and careerism.
   10. Friendship and brotherhood among peoples of the USSR; intolerance of national and racial hatred.
   11. An uncompromising attitude to the enemies of communism; peace and freedom of nations.
   12. Fraternal solidarity with the working people of all countries and with all peoples.[18]

A careful reading of this moral code strongly indicates two outstanding and contradictory characteristics. The condensed injunctions and prohibitions in principles 3, 4, 6, 7, 8, and 9 are neither original nor ideological in content. These moral principles are the integral elements of social relations in any civilized community and have endured for ages as universal values in the history of humankind. However, in the case of the Soviet moral code, these principles acquired a purely functional meaning, designed not only to maintain social relations but also to strengthen and solidify the Soviet social system. In the process, with his preferences predetermined, the "new Soviet man" was deprived of making his choices and the moral code succeeded in reducing morality to the simple transaction of carrying out orders, striving for a uniformity alien and hostile to individuality.

In contrast, questions arise with regard to the ideological provisions of principles 1, 2, 5, 10, 11, and 12, which utilize standards peculiar to Marxist-Leninist "truths" conceived in terms of hypothetical, long-range historical goals.

Charting the course of moral behavior, the Party ideologues presented themselves as the ultimate judges in all questions of good and evil, but in so doing they blurred the bonds of human association arbitrarily defined in the devotion to the Communist cause—supposedly the primary dimension of human existence. That is, in a collectivist society, with the Communist cause extolled as the highest ideal, the moral code divides the community of man into two hostile camps of "them" versus "us," locked in a deadly contest for the "victory of Communism." This narrowly focused view of humanity was clearly expressed in the Party Programme, which stated that there was "a grim struggle going on between two ideologies—Communist and bourgeois—in the world today."[19] Building its ethic on the premises of this struggle, the Communist Party, bent on the ideological orientation radically devoid of any element of all-human morality, dangerously polarized international relations and officially sanctioned a violently hostile attitude toward the political and spiritual world of the West.

However ideological and divisive the concept of "devotion to the Communist cause," it must not be considered in isolation from principle 11 of the moral code, which was a plea for an "uncompromising attitude to the enemies of communism." That this was an updated version of the old Bolshevik political canon of *kto kogo*—literally, "who will destroy whom"—was hardly noticed in Western studies of this *Moral Code for the Builder of Communism*. Based on its explanation of the class struggle as the driving force of history, Marxism perceived the development of society as a struggle between antagonistic classes, in which the bourgeoisie would eventually perish and the proletariat would ultimately emerge as a victor. In other words, if the proletarian class struggle was to be pursued to its ultimate end, matter-of-fact political action left no room for any compromise or accommodation, because, according to Lenin, "force alone settles the great problem of political liberty and the class struggle."[20] This glorification of violence was adapted and transformed by Lenin and his heirs into an operational code—a hard and fast rule for the party's political conduct, requiring an uncompromising attitude toward any political opponent. And since the backdrop of politics is essentially one of a continuous and irreconcilable conflict, the political opponent must be destroyed in order to expedite the process of history.[21]

It is clear that principles 1 and 11 of the moral code faithfully reflected the Bolshevik operational code. These two principles, bound together in a mutually supportive premise, supposedly leading to higher, more abstract normative values, in reality concealed—under the guise of a healthier individual and public morality—a carte blanche sanction of violent, unethical practices.[22] This Machiavellian schism in Communist ethics was described in idealistic and perfectionist terms in Soviet ethical literature, which simultaneously and unwittingly disclosed the true meaning and purpose of these two principles. Explaining and discussing the moral code, a collective of Soviet theoreticians wrote:

> When building Communism, the community prepares its citizens for it, cultivates noble qualities in them, assists them to root out everything which besmirches human dignity. This is a far more complicated business than would appear from certain utopian novels, in which no one explains whence the "ready made" Communists have sprung or whither everybody *disappeared* who does not fit the requirements of society.[23]

It must be added that, from the perspective of basic human rights, Soviet ethicists, so concerned with eradicating "everything that besmirches human dignity," were oblivious of the fact that the first principle of the moral code—calling for "devotion to the Communist cause"—actually constituted a surrender of human dignity, since this "moral" principle deprived man of his freedom of choice *not to profess* certain beliefs.[24] This attempt to impose an intolerant ideology on an entire people was justified by the socialist practice of fostering a "Communist consciousness" in every individual—presumably one of the Party's most important tasks in the process of Communist construction.[25] Thus people were "educated" and "prepared" for the acceptance of this socialist practice in which "the consciousness of separate individuals does not merely register the presence of principles and forms of organization of socialist society, but accepts them as a right and just system."[26] It is then that "*knowledge* becomes approval of the socialist principles and norms of social organization, becomes ideological convictions that guide people's actions towards consolidation and development of socialist society."[27]

Needless to say, the "cultivation of a Communist consciousness" was a euphemism for a consistent and unrelenting method of indoctrination in which beliefs (such as the party's history, its ideas, and its policy) were never to be questioned but were constantly and systematically hammered into the minds of every man, woman, and child, from kindergarten to factory, office, or institution. As if anticipating criticism, the Soviet theoretician Georgi Smirnov asserted that, according to history, even when there is a common ground on fundamental issues, leading to a uniformity of ideas and opinions within a society, there is still ample room for creative solutions to new problems.[28] Whether the basis for this assertion was a "general unity of basic principles" or a "community of fundamental interests on the scale of the whole society,"[29] it is obvious that, in the pre-Gorbachev era, the internal closure to novel ideas dispossessed the Soviet citizen of the right to make comparisons and curtailed his or her freedom to judge independently what was right or wrong in the competition of political ideas.

If a citizen's freedom of choice was easily dispensable in the name of Communist morality, the virtues of Soviet collectivism, with its guiding principle "all for one and one for all," constituted another step in the imposition of ideological and moral values, ensuring the peaceful acceptance of the monopolistic exercise of power by the Communist elite. Thus, in Soviet ethical literature, collectivism represented a fusion of society and the individual, who was considered an integral part of the collective and was expected to acquire the capacity to subordinate his or her personal interests to communal interests.[30] Moreover, the individual was conceived as having no real being outside the collective, since his "personal endeavor springs from the *urge* to do everything to enable the collective to successfully accomplish the job at hand, and it is this creative endeavor which adorns the collective."[31] This determination to build a "new man" promoted the illusion of the creative experience of collective innovation, because "the wider people's ties with the collective, the richer and more beautiful were their spiritual lives,"[32] and, as Soviet philosophers believed, "only in a collective does man develop and display his gifts and abilities to their fullest."[33] In contrast to these views, the results of some Western sociological studies on the interaction of individuals in complex organizational groups indicated that "the product of the 'best' individual is superior to that of the 'best' group."[34] Even the Soviet experience itself demonstrated the absence of virtues in the ideas of collectivism. The brutal and forceful collectivization of the peasantry in the 1930s, creating human suffering on an unprecedented scale, was still—sixty years later—a gross liability to the Soviet economic system.

Yet "the socialist system made collectivism the fundamental principle of social relations,"[35] and as the individual was submerged in the collective, he or she was presumably "consciously and voluntarily" subordinating personal interests to those of Soviet society, respecting the collective and its decisions, and fully aware of his or her responsibility to the collective.[36] Thus the moral code eliminated the "negative" aspects of individual freedom, replacing the traditional liberties—the right either to voice dissent or to organize political parties of a non-Communist persuasion—with the "positive" functions of socially useful labor. Within the realm of the all-embracing collective, the Soviet citizen was simply a component of the social organization—a part of an "ensemble of social relations" (this Marxist description of man was found in virtually every Soviet book on ethics), acting under conditions of restraint and censorship scrupulously enforced in the daily life of the Soviet citizen.

The dictatorial elite of the totalitarian society not only restricts freedom of information and prohibits dissent but defines the very content of the ideas that it imposes on its citizens. In retrospect, it is obvious that Khrushchev's successors discarded, for all practical purposes, the over-ambitious 1961 Party Programme but left intact the moral code. In truth, this code merited a more telling description as "twelve easy lessons in ethics and non-ethics." The strongly presented but vaguely formulated principles of the moral code served to facilitate a swing from a rather brief period of reforms and relaxation during the few years of the "thaw" to the more rigid and authoritarian policies that Isaac Deutscher described for lack of a better term as crypto- or neo-Stalinist.[37]

At the Twenty-fifth Congress of the Communist Party of the Soviet Union, fifteen years after the adoption of the moral code, the late L. I. Brezhnev, deeply dissatisfied with the state of inertia in Soviet social engineering, expressed his concern with the ideological, moral, and cultural levels of Soviet society. In his speech to the congress, he remonstrated the Soviet people saying that "gaps between word and deed, in whatever form they are expressed, are harmful to economic construction, but are particularly damaging to moral upbringing."[38] Furthermore, he complained that:

money-grubbing, private ownership tendencies, hooliganism, red tape and indifference to other people are at variance with the very essence of our system. In the struggle against such phenomena, it is necessary to make full use of the opinions of the workers' collectives, critical statements in the press, methods of persuasion, the force of law—of all the means at our disposal.[39]

Apparently, Brezhnev's words did not fall on deaf ears. Within a year after the Twenty-fifth Congress, the authors of a primer in Marxist-Leninist theory republished the entire moral code and commented on the collectivist morality in action, stating that "man's moral compass" in a socialist society is morality which "represents one of the most important means of social control."[40] The same approach—i.e., morality as social control—was the basic subject matter of a major article written by a leading Soviet theoretician (the chief editor of *Pravda*), V. G. Afanas'ev.[41] Undoubtedly inspired by Brezhnev's speech, Afanas'ev dedicated his article to "actual problems of modernity in light of the resolutions of the Twenty-fifth Congress."[42] Suggesting that society's moral conscience serves as an effective means of social control of individual human behavior, Afanas'ev examined the collective aspect of morality and questioned its legitimacy in controlling man and his behavior. Unhesitatingly, Afanas'ev declared that

> man is endowed with a will, a mind, and the ability to exercise conscious control over his thoughts and deeds; his exceptional and subtle mental qualities and his rich unique life make the very idea of outside intervention in man's affairs seem blasphemous. It is evident that the control of man is quite a different process than the control of a technical system or an assembly line in an industrial plant—man is not confined to one-way manipulation and assimilation. There is a multitude of controlling influences exerted on man through formal and informal channels, and direct or indirect means.[43]

Generally speaking, Soviet theoreticians, because of their strong belief in the collectivist idea, never spoke of a personal vision of man but always talked in terms of the group or for the sake of the collective. They never offered us any inkling of their doubts or ventured outside of the impersonal pronouncements in the Marxist-Leninist jargon with its incessant ideological casuistry. True to form, Afanas'ev, forgetting that he had just labeled as blasphemous the idea of controlling the individual, declared that man is, first and foremost, a social being—a product of society—and that therefore it is indisputable that society, in one way or another, controls individual development and behavior.[44]

Utterly disregarding the fact that human experience is too diffuse a phenomenon to be so easily controlled and repressed, Afanas'ev claimed that under socialism, one of the greatest tasks was the "truly scientific management of all components and elements in the social system, and above all, the control of the people."[45] He added that the success of communism was predicated on the extent to which people were trained to perform functions of various production-related, socio-political, and ideological tasks, refining the coordination of their resources and maximizing the effectiveness of industrial production. What seemed to matter most to Afanas'ev was the accuracy with which people measured their efforts against the standards established by social requirements, moral principles, and legal norms. What these standards were or how one arrived at achieving them Afanas'ev found unworthy of consideration. Instead, he turned his attention to the problems of developmental and behavioral control of the individual.

According to Afanas'ev, "to control the individual, one must determine his place in the social system, define his rights and duties, and ascertain his social function in a given collective or society."[46] As if to emphasize the collective's control over the individual, Afanas'ev claimed that the content and nature of social functions "are determined by the character of the social system and by the goals that society and its collectives set for themselves; the individual contributes to the fulfillment of the common goals and solution of problems through his performance of his social functions."[47] Thus the collective shapes the individual's plans in life and helps him or her to clarify possible ways and means to realize these plans. However, said Afanas'ev, "the behavior and the actions of the individual must be influenced in such a way that his social functions conform to the interests of society and the collective."[48]

To create the most promising conditions for the performance of the individual's social functions, Afanas'ev suggested that it was first necessary to ensure the individual's *adaptation* to the collective.[49] It was Afanas'ev's view that the process of adaptation was a very complex process which consisted of four closely interrelated components:

> 1) Physical and psychological adaptation to working conditions, which include: technology, the state of sanitation and hygiene, multiple workshifts, degree of nervous and physical strain, etc. 2) Psychological adaptation—the individual's internal adaptability to the demands of the organization; state of mental stability, including satisfaction with the job and the working conditions. 3) Sociopsychological interpersonal adaptation—adaptability to the other members of the collective, to colleagues, supervisors, and the collective as a whole. 4) Social adapta-

tion in the narrow sense of the term—the individual's acceptance of the collective's norms, values and standards of behavior.[50]

For Afanas'ev, morality was not that aspect of life which most basically determines its quality but was, rather, an ethic of blind obedience or submission to a collectivist moral code imposed from above. It seemed that the elusiveness of a sensitive, analytic content in Soviet ethical literature was due to the ideological belief that a theory must be judged not by its correspondence to facts but by the extent to which it was in agreement with the fundamental principles of Marxism-Leninism. This curious mixture of doctrine, theory, and dogma was the most conspicuous feature of Soviet ethical and political writings, beginning with serious Marxist-Leninist studies and ending with the Party Programme and its ubiquitous moral code.

True to this ideological style of ethical and political discourse, Afanas'ev's collectivist approach to the control of the individual represents a classic example of Richard W. Wilson's comprehensive analysis of the closed social and political environment in a totalitarian society.[51] According to Wilson, autonomy training of an individual in a closed society produces sociocentric attitudes and identification, with a consequent reliance on situations predetermined by the collective. This, in turn, leads to a rigidity of moral training as the individual is indoctrinated into ethnocentric, group-oriented values. The emotions of the individual in a closed society are manipulated through fear, shame, and guilt, with the individual totally dependent on the group. For feedback regarding his or her behavior, the individual is restricted to only one socially approved channel, that is, the state and its dominating ideology.[52]

Afanas'ev saw in the process of adaptation and in the work performance of the individual only a test of morality reduced to social responsibility, thereby eliminating in one stroke the ethical decision as a distinctly private, individualized view of humanity and the world. Afanas'ev asked man to identify himself with a set of universal, collectivist ideals and demanded that man, in the name of these ideals, offer everything in return for the promise that "Communism would bring an abundance of material and spiritual values, thus creating conditions for their happiness."[53]

Because only work could produce the promised abundance of material and spiritual values and the condition of happiness, the idea of socially useful labor determined the social status of the Soviet citizen. Soviet ethicists repeatedly spoke of the redemptive value of labor in molding the "new Soviet man." According to the moral code, productive, conscientious labor became a moral obligation, and one's very recognition in society depended primarily on one's participation in the construction of communism.

However, there was quite a gap between these optimistic, self-righteous assumptions and the actual conditions of Soviet society. Soviet social reality was obscured by ideological slogans such as "work is the source of inspiration and spiritual uplift" and "the new Soviet man was tempered by labor."[54] These slogans reflected the function of historical materialism—to observe, analyze, and provide various means to change and improve the workings of man and society—and were applied in Soviet practice with a propagandistic twist: the shabby present was virtually ignored and the future was treated as if it had already arrived.

In sharp contrast to this ideological smokescreen was the fact that the Soviet worker was reduced to a functional unit—to an extension of the collective form of labor. It was this extension of the collective form of labor that "made demands on personal qualities such as team spirit, comradely mutual assistance, good organization and discipline, and an ability to put the interests of the whole collective above one's own."[55] It was not always recognized in the West that the Soviet workers' views were carefully prescribed from above, and any individual manifestations of a political and moral character were simply not tolerated. "Workbooks" issued to every worker, into which merits, demerits, promotions, demotions, and so forth were inscribed, served as a means of controlling the worker's free choice of employment.[56] The Soviet worker had no right to any collective action, such as a work stoppage or a strike, to register dissatisfaction with the working conditions. The worker's unions were labor unions in name only, since most of the union activity at the factory level (including the setting of output norms and wages) was tightly controlled by the local party organization. And, finally, despite a depressed living standard, the Soviet worker was working much longer and harder for lower wages than his or her Western counterpart. Workers' committees were frowned upon and the Communist elite would never allow a worker to take part in the decision-making process, much less let a worker participate in the running of production plants or other state enterprises.

The glorification of labor and praises of its redemptive value could not conceal the low productivity of the Soviet workers and their lifestyle in an economy of chronic scarcity stood in sharp contrast to the high social status of the Communist elite, who had somehow managed to secure considerable privileges in representing the "best" interests of the proletariat and peasantry. It is true the Communist Party professed some concern for the general welfare of the people. Acting in this vein, the "leading and guiding" force of Soviet society proposed in its Party Programme the elimination of socio-economic and cultural distinctions between town and country, with the intent of narrowing wage and income differentials that were strikingly at odds with the commitment of attaining a classless society. Still preserving the social distance between the elite and the rank and file, a number of modest reforms took place in the 1961–1970 period. While these reforms included a drive toward greater egalitarianism on the socio-economic level, as Mervyn Matthews observed, if these reforms "did not produce an even more equal distribution of income, it is because it must have been opposed by some very powerful forces."[57] It seems that with the system of stratification in Soviet society, the idea of "comradely mutual assistance" combined with the "one for all and all for one" principle of the moral code were of little consequence. These principles camouflaged the overwhelming tendencies toward social differentiation and the conspicuous disparities in economic rewards that existed under the conditions of "advanced socialism."

The promulgation of the moral code did not add new dimensions to the discussions of morality in Soviet philosophy. The great majority of Soviet philosophers—as a rule, highly skilled in reacting and adapting themselves to the "party line" or other specific directives—accepted the moral code without any protest or criticism. Why Soviet philosophers, moored in the Marxist-Leninist system of "absolute truths," displayed an incapacity to take a longer view of life and failed to question human conduct and beliefs in the overall framework of Soviet reality is the subject matter of the next chapter.

Notes

1. V. I. Lenin, "The Immediate Tasks of the Soviet Government" (April 1918), in *Selected Works*, vol. 2 (New York: International Publishers, 1967), 664.

2. A slightly altered version of this chapter appeared as Sigmund Krancberg, "Controlling Individual Development and Behavior," *Studies in Soviet Thought* 27 (1984): 319-34, © 1984 by D. Reidel Publishing Company; reprinted here by permission of Kluwer Academic Publishers.

3. The 26th Congress of the Communist Party of the Soviet Union, *Documents and Resolutions* (Moscow: Novosti Press Agency Publishing House, 1981), 101.

4. Ibid.

5. Ibid.

6. Richard T. De George, *Soviet Ethics and Morality* (Ann Arbor: University of Michigan Press, 1969).
7. Richard T. De George, "Soviet Ethics and Soviet Society," *Studies in Soviet Thought* 4 (1964): 207.
8. Cited in Philip T. Grier, *Marxist Ethical Theory in the Soviet Union* (Boston and Dordrecht: D. Reidel Publishing Co., 1978), 88.
9. Ibid.
10. Ibid., 98.
11. M. Rosenthal and P. Yudin, eds., *Dictionary of Philosophy* (Moscow: Progress Publishers, 1967).
12. Ibid., 98.
13. Ibid.
14. The editors of the *Dictionary of Philosophy* also failed to offer the etymological explanation of the linguistic origins of the words "ethics" and "morals." "Ethics" is derived from the Greek word *ethos*, meaning "character" and, in the plural, "manners," whereas "morals" derives from the Latin *moralis*, which also means "character" or manners. In philosophical discourse, ethics and morals are often used interchangeably, although a number of philosophers have suggested clear distinctions between the two concepts.
15. Grier, *Marxist Ethical Theory*, 96.
16. *Programme of the Communist Party of the Soviet Union* (Moscow: Foreign Languages Publishing House, 1961), 54. (Of course, the Kremlin bigwigs did not foresee that in the 1980s the Soviet empire would move rapidly toward its dissolution.)
17. Ibid., 100.
18. Ibid., 100-101.
19. Ibid., 41.
20. V. I. Lenin, *Two Tactics of Social Democracy in the Democratic Revolution,* in *Selected Works*, vol. 1, 469.
21. Alexander L. George, "The Operational Code: A Neglected Approach to the Study of Political Leaders and Decision-Making," *International Studies Quarterly* 13 (1969): 191-221.
22. N. Leites, *Operational Code of the Politburo* (Santa Monica, Calif.: The Rand Corporation, 1951).
23. Georgi Shakhnazarov et al., eds., *Man, Science, and Society* (Moscow: Progress Publishers, 1965), 241. Emphasis added. Henceforth referred to as *Man*.
24. Most societies, of course, endeavor to inculcate their ruling principles and demand at least a ritual profession of faith in the official creed. But the Soviet regime—in the pre-Gorbachev era—carried this demand to extraordinary lengths and with extraordinary force, virtually seeking to obliterate any sphere of private or personal autonomy. Any regime that respects human dignity must have at least some regard for the privacies of society and the soul; in liberal democracies, of course, that regard ranks among the first principles of politics.
25. George Smirnov, *Soviet Man: The Making of a Socialist Type of Personality* (Moscow: Progress Publishers, 1973), 21-29.

26. Ibid., 174.
27. Ibid. Emphasis added.
28. Ibid., 287.
29. Ibid.
30. *Man*, 254–55.
31. Ibid.
32. Ibid., 256.
33. Rosenthal and Yudin, eds., *Dictionary of Philosophy*, 83.
34. E. Michael Bannester, *Relevance and Power: The Elemental Sociodynamics* (London: Center of Sociodynamics, 1971), 136.
35. Smirnov, *Soviet Man*, 164.
36. Rosenthal and Yudin, eds., *Dictionary of Philosophy*, 83.
37. *50 Years of Communism in Russia*, ed. Milorad Drachkovitch (University Park: Pennsylvania State University Press, 1968), 8.
38. *Current Soviet Policies* (The Documentary Record of the 25th Congress of the Communist Party of the Soviet Union) (Columbus, Ohio: American Association of Slavic Studies, 1976), 28.
39. Ibid.
40. G. K. Shakhnazarov, A. D. Boborykin, et al., eds., *Social Science* (Moscow: Progress Publishers, 1977), 438.
41. V. G. Afanas'ev, "Controlling Individual Development and Behavior," *Voprosy filosofii* 11 (1976): 3–15. Cf. *The Soviet Review* 20, no. 3 (Fall 1979): 15–37.
42. Ibid., 3.
43. Ibid.
44. Ibid.
45. Ibid.
46. Ibid., 5.
47. Ibid., 6.
48. Ibid., 8.
49. It is noteworthy that in the first years of *glasnost*, the ideal of a collectivist upbringing was still considered as one of the highest principles of communist morality. (*Problemy nauchnovo kommunisma*, Vypusk 19 [Problems of Scientific Communism, Issue 19] [Moscow, 1987]: 113.)
50. Ibid., 8.
51. Richard W. Wilson, "Political Socialization and Moral Development," *World Politics* 33, 153–77.
52. Ibid., 171–77.
53. *Man*, 241.
54. Ibid., 250.
55. L. Blyakhman and O. Shkaratan, *Man at Work* (Moscow: Progress Publishers, 1977), 237.
56. Michael Rywkin, *Soviet Society Today* (London: M. E. Sharpe, 1989), 142.
57. Mervyn Matthews, *Class and Society in Soviet Russia* (New York: Walker & Co., 1972), 78.

5

Soviet Philosophy

> There is no greater danger to human liberty than dogma, the monopoly of one group, one ideology, one system.
>
> Sir Ralph Dahrendorf, *Reflections on the Revolution in Europe*

Major schools of Western philosophy go about their business in an atmosphere of prudent and precise reasoning, expressed in meaningful but austere language. This attitude is further joined by a passion for clarity and a steadfast dedication to objectivity, which set the rules for the most dispassionate manner of discourse. Problems of philosophy are analyzed, dissected, refined, and reduced to logical constructs and if found wanting in the light of this scrutiny, are declared intellectually worthless and refused any recognition whatsoever.

It therefore becomes difficult to present an exposition of philosophy as it was practiced in the Soviet Union, where philosophy, "a science of the general laws of being (i.e., nature and society), human thinking, and the process of knowledge,"[1] was never fully separated from ideology. In one sense, ideology in the Soviet Union was considered a conglomerate of false rationalizations of the bourgeois ruling classes, used for the purpose of justifying and preserving the political and economic relations of capitalist society. In another sense, the use of the term "ideology" related to a system of views and ideas applied to the interpretation of Soviet experience and was manifested in a total commitment to the practices and institutions emanating from the Communist Party. Hence, a plausible and clear presentation of Soviet philosophy is not so much complicated by the habitual and tedious expressions of self-righteousness or by the expectations of the supposedly inevitable communist utopia, as it is confused by the overall ideological tone of philosophy in the former Soviet Union.

Observing the currents of philosophy in the Soviet Union before the advent of *glasnost* and *perestroika*, one perceives at once its dual and contradictory nature. On the one hand, philosophy in the Soviet Union was undoubtedly elevated to a stronger position than in any other country. On the other hand, the same philosophy, interchangeably labeled as dialectical materialism or Marxism-Leninism, had acquired a distinctly one-sided political and dogmatic character, designed not only to express and support the ideological aims of the Soviet Communist Party but also to exercise a determining influence over the structure and style of philosophical endeavor in the Soviet Union.

It was Lenin who pointed out that

> recent philosophy is as partisan as philosophy was two thousand years ago. In other words, today as in the past, the philosophers are divided into two mutually opposed camps, materialism and idealism. In the final analysis, the struggle between them is an expression of the tendencies and ideologies of opposed social groups and classes.[2]

This so-called party principle (*partiynost*) claimed that in a class society philosophy could not be nonpartisan, and that essentially it reflected in its views the ideology and the specific interests of the class it served. Moreover, according to this cardinal principle of Soviet philosophy, opposition to Marxism-Leninism not only was a response to a deep emotional commitment to bourgeois class interests but also was demonstrated in the reactionary nature of Western philosophy, which, in its theories, downgraded or disregarded the real import of social struggle. The presupposition of the social struggle rested on the assertion that capitalist society was divided and deeply troubled by the antagonistic confrontation between the oppressing and oppressed classes. The Soviet philosophers believed that the oppressed, meaning the lower working classes of capitalist society, were in turn committed to the cause of ending exploitation, struggling and striving for the ideals of socialism and communism.

After the victory of the October Revolution, Soviet philosophy not only accepted without question the "party principle," but also adapted Lenin's political and polemical style. This led to an impatience with complexity, to the insistence on bringing everything down to a single issue, to the conjuration of "objective" conditions, and to an unscrupulous readiness to distort the position of the opponent. Above all, the attempt to simplify and to reduce all philosophical controversies to the common denominator of a conflict between materialism and idealism cynically obscured, rather than clarified, issues and problems.

The establishment of the Institute of Red Professors and the Communist Academy in the early post-revolutionary period was seen not as a comprehensive attempt to control intellectual life but as an organized and effective means of propagating Marxism-Leninism in intellectual circles. However, in 1921, with the start of a serious campaign against religion and against "idealistic" tendencies, the majority of non-Marxist professors, including some of the more prominent academic philosophers, were removed from their teaching positions.

Still, Soviet philosophers—now Marxist-Leninists in their great majority—did not suffer from strict edicts of official dogma or from the complete authoritarian control that was to be established with the consolidation of the Stalinist regime in 1929.

It is true that communism in the early 1920s gave serious treatment to the problems of securing the ideological and material foundations of a new proletarian culture. Nevertheless, there was a great degree of freedom in the heated polemics of the day. Soviet philosophers disagreed about the status of philosophy and initiated discussions on important aspects of the dialectic and dialectical materialism.

One of the most debated topics among Communist writers centered on the question of the very existence of philosophy. According to Plekhanov and Lenin, philosophy was a very important branch of learning and, as such, was an integral part of Marxism, which derived its foundation from a creative, materialist development of the Hegelian dialectic. Another group, consisting mostly of natural scientists, insisted that Marxism, as the only true doctrine, simply eliminated traditional philosophy and heralded the advent of science. The most outspoken representative of this group, S. K. Minin, aired his antiphilosophical views in an essay "Filosofiya za bort" (Overboard with Philosophy). Another member of this group of "mechanists," Stepanov-Skvortsov, in one of his works stated: "The Marxist recognizes no special field of philosophical activity from that of science; for the Marxist, materialist philosophy consists in the latest and most general findings of modern science."[3]

For some time, mechanist conceptions, based on a simplistic scientific optimism, were quite popular in Soviet intellectual circles, in the years from 1922 to 1926. However, the mechanists were strongly opposed by a number of Soviet philosophers later known as the "Menshevizing idealists." The most prominent among them was A. M. Deborin, who developed his views in the controversy with the mechanists and who based his arguments on the philosophical works of Plekhanov.[4] In his struggle with the mechanists, Deborin stressed the independent status of philosophy (dialectical materialism) over and above the natural sciences: "Dialectical materialism exists as an independent discipline alongside the other positive sciences, more especially as the methodology and theory of scientific knowledge."[5]

Moreover, Deborin accused the mechanists of neglecting the unique character of the specific levels or stages in the development of matter (being-life-consciousness) and thus eliminating the basic modes of categories of being.

In the end, the views of the Deborinists prevailed. Aided by the Communist ideological tradition and by a number of pronouncements of doctrinal authority from leading Bolsheviks, mechanism was declared out of step with the achievements of modern science and branded as an unwelcome digression from the basic tenets of Marxism-Leninism.

It is noteworthy that Deborin was one of the first Soviet philosophers who strongly criticized *History and Class Consciousness*, published by Lukacs in 1923. A year later, Deborin accused Lukacs of a revisionist attempt to interpret Marx by discarding Engels. According to Deborin, the two classic authors of Marxism are inseparable, and a close reading of their works will not reveal any appreciable disagreement between them.

However, the victory of the Deborinists over the mechanists was short-lived. In an important speech on September 27, 1929, Stalin again condemned the mechanists but at the same time attacked Soviet philosophical theoreticians in general. This speech was the beginning of an organized campaign against the relatively free style of philosophical discourse in the Soviet Union. While mechanism was said to be a right-wing deviation that readily served the interests of the *kulak*[6] agents within the party, Deborinism was condemned for supposedly giving support to Trotsky's "left-wing deviation," or Menshevizing idealism. Furthermore, Deborinists were accused of being overly abstract, of misunderstanding the significance of the relation between theory and practice, and of divorcing philosophy from politics. Deborin was personally taken to task for valuing Hegel too highly and for obscuring the differences between Hegel and Marx. Above all, Deborin was attacked for remaining aloof from the great tasks and challenges of socialist construction.

About two years later, the Central Committee of the Communist Party officially denounced mechanism and Deborinism, once more singling out Deborin and his comrades for dangerous distortions of Marxism-Leninism. Shortly thereafter, Deborin publicly admitted that he had fallen into the deplorable errors of Menshevizing idealism and that his philosophy, suffering from serious neglect of the Leninist Party principles, was divorced from concrete life. In his recantation, Deborin thanked the Central Committee and especially Comrade Stalin for correcting him and restraining him from the errant ways.[7]

This decree of the Central Committee of the Communist Party on January 25, 1931, marked the beginning of a new era in Soviet philosophy. From this day on, every effort was directed at keeping the work of philosophy in the closest possible contact with the life and program of the party. In turn, this new trend virtually assured the Communist Party of steady and unwavering philosophical support in its political struggle to impose the Stalinist party line. At the same time, Soviet philosophy gave prominence not only to Marx, Engels, and Lenin, but also, to a great degree, to Stalin. The period of lively discussion characterizing the preceding years (1917–1930) was a matter of the past. With it disappeared the last vestiges of pre-revolutionary traditions and culture, followed by a Stalinist dictatorship that demanded and enforced the complete subordination of philosophical activity to the authority of the Communist Party of the Soviet Union (CPSU). Philosophical knowledge and a critical approach to theoretical problems did not count any more as outstanding qualities. What mattered was the readiness to conform to the dictates of the party. In other words, the allegiance to a doctrinaire world outlook blended with the single philosophical school of institutionalized Marxist theory, narrowed the choice of general perspectives, and imposed a number of conditioning factors in strict conformity with the party line.

This was the beginning of the long period of silence in Soviet philosophy, which was interrupted only by the submissive chatter of sycophants. The only controversies permitted in the philosophical realm were directed against bourgeois ideologies; any other discussions among Soviet philosophers usually touched upon internal "heresies" and ideological errors, followed by the inevitable disclaimers and humiliating recantations.

The new course of Soviet philosophy was forcefully directed into a rigid mold of officially prescribed opinions, with Stalin elevated to the status of fountainhead of all wisdom. Philosophers, subservient in every respect to the requirements of the party, competed among themselves in trying to give the impression that there was only one creative philosopher in the Soviet Union—Comrade Stalin. The leading official Soviet philosopher in the 1930s, M. B. Mitin—a member of the Soviet Academy of Sciences and the Central Committee of the CPSU—wrote:

> The further advancement of Marxist-Leninist theory in every department, including that of the philosophy of Marxism, is associated with the name of Comrade Stalin. In all Comrade Stalin's practical achievements, and in all his writings, there is set forth the whole experience

of the worldwide struggle of the proletariat, the whole rich storehouse of Marxist-Leninist theory.[8]

In his subsequent publications, Mitin's obsequiousness found its outlet in the glorification of the Communist Party of the Soviet Union—the most "genuine source of wisdom."[9] As a matter of fact, in October of 1961, the Soviet philosopher P. I. Shabalkin, who spent twenty years in prisons and concentration camps, accused Mitin of criminal complicity in the Stalinist purges of 1930s. Although this accusation was serious and well documented, it was completely ignored by Soviet authorities. Their only reaction was absolute official silence in this case.[10]

In 1936, there was another upheaval in Soviet philosophy. The new Stalinist constitution was proclaimed as a great and historic achievement, marking the end of the construction period of the foundations of socialism. The Soviet people were told that they had successfully reached the stage of socialism and that they were about to embark on the splendid road to communism. All this was taking place in the grim climate of mass purges, with Communist publications full of pious pronouncements on the significance of socialist legality and the importance of the individual in the new Soviet society.

At the same time, Soviet philosophers (including Mitin) were again taken to task for presenting to the public philosophical works of abstract and scholastic tendencies. The Stalinists labeled many philosophers as political illiterates for merely mentioning the works of Trotsky, Bukharin, and Zinoviev, who were exposed at the famous Moscow Trials. As expected, Mitin and his colleagues publicly acknowledged their errors and meekly promised to follow the party line from then on. With the party relentlessly attacking any independent and original work, philosophical activity in the Soviet Union virtually came to a standstill. The only remaining Soviet philosophical journal, *Under the Banner of Marxism*, even ceased publication in 1944.

After the Second World War, the year 1947 marked the end of the long period of silence in Soviet philosophy. However, the trend of renewed philosophical activity was nonetheless circumscribed within the narrow channels of the Stalinist "model" of philosophical endeavor—the party was still considered the final authority on all philosophical and scientific questions. Instead of the hoped-for relaxation of political control, there was an intensified concern with ideology and its influence in philosophy.

Still, in 1947, the journal *Voprosy filosofii* (Problems of Philosophy) began publication. In the same year, it was decreed that formal logic should be taught in all higher academic institutions. (In the 1930s, formal logic was dismissed as a "metaphysical habit of thought.") The output of philosophical works increased considerably. The stress on the significance of the party principle, with its emphasis on party fidelity, was more and more pronounced. Zhdanov, Stalin's Minister of Culture, attacked one of the leading Soviet philosophers, G. F. Aleksandrov, for bourgeois "objectivism" and abstract neutrality in his work. Ironically, before this attack, Aleksandrov was elected to the General Assembly of the Academy of Sciences in 1946 and was highly praised as a "Stalin Prize winner, Head of the Propaganda and Agitation Section of the Central Committee of the Communist Party of the Soviet Union, Professor of the history of philosophy in the Academy of Social Sciences . . . a gifted exponent of Marxist-Leninist philosophy."[11]

The vagueness and triviality of the official accusations directed against Aleksandrov can only be interpreted as a new attempt by the Central Committee to launch an attack on the "philosophical front" with the purpose of setting stricter ground rules for philosophical work. The tone of the campaign underscored ideological dedication and devotion to the party—Zhdanov singled out Aleksandrov for the nonpolitical character of his work, for its remoteness from contemporary issues, and for the lack of a militant Bolshevik Party spirit. Zhdanov went on to say that Stalin was, in general, dissatisfied with the work of Soviet philosophers, because they displayed too much timidity and abstractness.[12]

Despite the usual wave of recantations, the new philosophical journal *Voprosy filosofii*, under the editorship of B. M. Kedrov, contained some notable essays that demonstrated a degree of originality and independence. However, in 1948, Kedrov was removed from his editorial post and the journal published the essay "Za Bolshevistskuyu Partiynost' v Filosofii" (For a Bolshevik Partisanship in Philosophy), in which it stated that some of the articles in *Voprosy filosofii* raised "questions which are not open to dispute" and "sought to revise the positions of Marxism-Leninism in relation to the history of Russian social thought."[13]

The campaign against ideological retardation in philosophy spread into other fields. Biologists, composers, linguists, writers, and even statisticians were sternly rebuked for the lack of ideological steadfastness and dedication manifested in the neglect of Marxist-Leninist dialectics.

Only the death of Stalin slowed down this campaign. Within a year, most references to Stalin as a philosophical genius virtually disappeared. There was a growing demand for honest, professional competence and integrity in philosophical work. This new trend was further helped by the twentieth Party Congress, which inaugurated the campaign for liquidating the cult of personality in Soviet political and cultural life. For once, Stalin's errors were not only publicly discussed but also criticized outright, and his readiness to make dogmatic statements in fields in which he was not competent was finally exposed. This was important progress in Soviet philosophy, which was still controlled by the party, but permitted a relatively free discussion without the threat of intimidations and recantations.

Gradually, especially after the twentieth Party Congress, there was a marked qualitative improvement in the style and composition of Soviet philosophy. To begin with, Einstein's theory of relativity, formerly declared unsound and inconsistent with the "objectivity of knowledge"—Soviet philosophers surmised that a bourgeois physicist such as Einstein could not come up with a valid theory—was, after prolonged discussions, officially accepted as compatible with the doctrines and views of dialectical materialism. At about the same time, cybernetics, roundly condemned as a reactionary pseudoscience, was accepted as a legitimate science of computers. In the mid-1960s, the Moscow University Philosophy Faculty ordered that formal and symbolic logic be taught separately from dialectical logic.[14]

All these developments created a significant change in all areas of Soviet philosophical activity. Nevertheless, the great majority of Soviet philosophers were still concerned with problems within the ideological structure of dialectical materialism, and their arguments were based on the "scientific" and "progressive" principles of Marxism-Leninism, which, over the years, acquired a canonical character.

But what were these essential principles of Marxism-Leninism, stripped of their ideological components which were mixed with the artificial and, at times, clumsy transplant of Hegelian dialectics?

Soviet philosophers believed that the actual primacy of matter is the most essential feature of reality. The three dominant properties of matter, motion, space, and time, are the inseparable elements of our material world. The whole world is an unlimited assortment of matter, which is apparent in a great many manifestations. The boundless varieties of matter, known in common usage as "things," while forming an integral whole, are in their infinite diversity dependent on and determined by each other. Besides the common properties and relations, things in the material world are also undergoing a continuous and unending process of change and development.

The diversity and unity of all things in the process of their existence are reflected in uniform laws, such as magnetism and gravitation, whose consistency and universality attest to the substantiality of the physical universe.

According to Soviet philosophers, dialectical materialism—the "scientific" philosophical world outlook and basic component of the Marxist doctrine—firmly believes in the unity of matter and consciousness. Dialectical materialism "proceeds from the fact that consciousness is a property not of any matter but of 'highly organized matter'."[15] In the long chain of evolution, the highest development of the brain originated and was achieved in human beings. Consciousness is the enterprise and creativity of the human brain in its coordinated connection with the nervous and sensory systems. The unity of matter and consciousness is further demonstrated in the most essential activity of the brain: in the perception of the external world. Fundamentally, perception is accomplished through a faithful reflection (the copy theory) of the outside world of matter in types of mental activity known as sensation, feeling, cognition, comprehension, and thought.

It is important to note that while Soviet philosophers believed in the unity of matter and consciousness, they were careful to stress the fact that matter and consciousness are not identical.

In practice, dialectical materialism was not only concerned with the study and interpretation of material phenomena; it was at the same time closely observing, analyzing, and providing various means to change and improve the workings of man and society. This sociological approach originated in the works of Marx and Engels, who claimed that the structure of society and the history of humanity have their bases in economic causation. In other words, it is a given set of material conditions at a given particular time that determines the course of history. This extension of dialectical materialism to the study of society and its history is the substance of historical materialism.

According to Soviet philosophers, the world of matter and motion undergoing the continuous process of change is subject to known general uniform laws. The process itself is of a strictly mechanical nature, since consciousness, motive, and will are not participants in purely natural phenomena. History, however, is made by people who have a great variety of tasks and aims, who constantly struggle for their fulfillment. The manner in which they go about satisfying their many tasks and aims not only determines the character of society but also sets its historical perspective.

Soviet philosophers held that if there is to be social life at all, humans have to procure, first of all, material resources that will satisfy their hunger, their thirst, and their need for shelter. To do this, they have to engage in labor activities that produce the necessary basic requirements and comforts of life. This steadily progressing process depends primarily on human beings' ability to control their physical environment, as well as on the degree of their mastery over the forces of nature. To satisfy their material needs in a more efficient manner, humans invent, make, and use all kinds of tools, ranging from the primitive implements of the Stone Age to the highly sophisticated machine aggregates of our century. The means of production created by humans, the tools and machines employed in this process, and above all the people involved in the process of production form the *productive forces of society*. "While the means of labor are the *determining* element in the productive forces," Soviet philosophers emphasized that the "working people, with their knowledge and experience, are the *most important* productive forces of society."[16]

The fact that production is basic to social life is not only reflected in the interaction between humans and nature but also in the relations between people who take part in production. On the whole, these production relations are founded on the relationship of the people to means of production—machines, land, raw materials, factory buildings, and so forth. Consequently, the character of the production relations—"depends on how the means of production are distributed in a society or, in other words, how the problem of the *ownership of the basic means of production* has been solved in that society."[17] Viewed from the economic perspective, it is the nature of these production relations that determines the dominant or subordinate role of various social groups in a given historical period.

According to Soviet philosophers, the production forces and the production relations—in their concrete aspects—constitute the mode of production. Generally speaking, the analysis of the mode of production "entails discovering what the productive forces and production relations are and how they are interconnected."[18] Historical materialism considers the productive forces and production relations as the two constantly changing elements in the mode of production. Unity and common purpose seem to be the characteristics of a given mode of production in its initial stages, but then the productive forces—meaning labor, production skills, and technology—make constant progress, while the production relations remain basically unchanged within the bounds of the mode of production. The lack of mobility in the production relations and their prospective retardation bring them into an ultimate conflict with the forces of production, which is sooner or later resolved in a "revolutionary destruction of the old, obsolete, and hidebound economic, social and political forms, which opens the road for the establishment of a new mode of production."[19] At this stage, the outdated production relations are replaced by new production relations that conform more closely to the nature of the forces of production.

According to Marxist-Leninist philosophers, the mode of production is the most essential form of development of society and is the basic determinant of society's economic structure. From the historical perspective, it is the economic structure that shapes and forms the groundwork for all other social relations in the political, cultural, legal, philosophical, moral, religious, and scientific fields of human endeavor. The ideas, organizations, and institutions of society, even the state itself, take their origin from this groundwork and constitute the superstructure of society. The general view of historical materialism is that this theory explains the inner workings of society as revealed in the mode of production and its connection to socio-economic relations, which in turn determine all other aspects of social life. It is the pervasive socio-economic formations that command the process of history, and according to Soviet philosophers, it is the theory of dialectical materialism and its scientific interpretation of history that provide man with knowledge of the general laws of development of society. In other words, Soviet philosophers believed that historical materialism, employing the dialectical method,[20] is capable of a concrete analysis of a given situation and of a correct assessment of historical events, taking into consideration most of the essential features of social phenomena along with the conditions, as well as the circumstances, of conflict and struggle. This "correct assessment of historic events" was not a Marxist-Leninist presupposition still to be tested and verified but a dogmatic belief open to confirmation but not to disproval. From this viewpoint, the Soviet approach to developments in Western society failed to take notice of the complexities of modern capitalism, with its concentration of managerial power in corporate form, and the growing influence of the state in the economic process. Most important, it paid insufficient attention to the integration of the working class into a social system it was supposed to undermine and destroy. Still, according to Soviet philosophers, the historical process, with its dialectical forcefulness, demonstrated the inevitability (consistent with the conclusions of historical materialism) of the eventual replacement of the capitalist socio-economic system with a socialist, and later a Communist, order. Needless to say, Soviet theoreticians further believed that the doctrines of dialectical and historical materialism represented the notion of ultimate truth in Marxist-Leninist philosophy, even if this notion combined cognitive and ideological functions in theory and practice.

Revolution is not only an attempt to change the social and economic order; it is at the same time an important moment in history, which brings forth a change in language, a new mode of thought, and a new social sense of values and ideas. Since the emergence of the Soviet state, the great majority of Soviet philosophers, following the tenets of Marxism-Leninism, aimed at a single, unified philosophy that would best express the essence and the concepts of dialectical and historical materialism. True to the famous dictum of Karl Marx that the task of the philosopher is not only to interpret the world but also to change it, the Soviet regime resolved to employ these theories as a blueprint and a program for converting the populace to the Soviet system, demonstrating at the same time a flexibility that could accommodate the currents of change and development. The indoctrination of Marxism-Leninism, with its expedient and, at times, brutal application of power aimed at socially and politically desired ends, exerted an equally enormous influence in conditioning and shaping Soviet thought. The success of the October Revolution, the sudden change from a revolutionary social movement into a state power structure dedicated to the construction of a "socialist order," served in itself as proof of the correctness of the philosophy of Marxism.

Hence, Marxism-Leninism acquired a prominence that made it the only accepted school of thought, and Marx, Engels, and Lenin became the undisputed "classics" of this school. Thus not only did Marxism-Leninism, also known in Soviet philosophy as dialectical and historical materialism, set the traditional and ideological formulae for an all-encompassing world view, but its central ideas became the foundation for all learning, research, and cultural, social, and political activity. At the same time, the Soviet regime attempted to turn this philosophy into a mass ideology. Soviet textbooks on dialectical and historical materialism were published in hundreds of thousands of copies[21] in editions reprinted every few years. However, the primitive and artless treatment of this difficult subject only contributed to the strengthening of a doctrinaire dogmatism displayed, at times, with religious fervor.

Consequently, Marxist-Leninist philosophy was developed and applied to the whole range of human thought and experience in the Soviet Union. With the massive impact of this philosophy, its ideas, concepts, and terminology found widespread use in the propagandist jargon of the party bureaucracy; in the educational system; in textbooks, speeches, literature, journals, and newspapers; and in the other media. In addition, Marxism-Leninism gained almost universal acceptance in the Soviet Union with the claim that it provided the framework for a scientific world view based on theories that were scientifically conclusive according to the laws of nature and history. Even in the absence of disciplined intellectual activity, this claim to scientific validity acquired universal acceptance in Soviet philosophy, manifested in the frequent disregard for scholarly truth. Inevitably, the outcome resulted in the formation of a general conviction that tended to reject the validity of any assertion merely because it contradicted the orthodox and ideological premises of dialectical and historical materialism.

Still, Soviet philosophers maintained that they subscribed to a "consistent commitment in philosophy which calls for a creative approach to theory"—a commitment supposedly demonstrated in the spirit of the "inalienable Marxist tradition."[22] By contrast, Soviet philosophers firmly believed that the destiny of mankind would lie in the downfall of capitalism, a contingent event at best, with the bourgeoisie forcibly giving up the private ownership of the instruments of production and the positions of command. This argument was reinforced by the automatic conclusion that the functions fulfilled by the bourgeoisie must be taken over by a revolutionary and victorious proletariat.

Soviet philosophers repeatedly emphasized the significance of the incessant ideological class struggle and its end result, proletarian power. They simply overlooked the fact that proletarians in power were no longer proletarians. In reality, once in power, the proletarian as a political person became superfluous. Proletarians in power had to delegate this power to their self-appointed representative, the Communist Party, which wielded autocratic rule through a centrally controlled political and economic system. The Communist Party was the ruling elite, which acted in the name of the whole society and professed some concern for its general welfare. While this perspective of general welfare was seriously handicapped by a life of constant scarcity, hardship, and economic shortcomings, the party elite managed to secure considerable privileges in representing the "best" interests of the proletariat. Just like the ordinary proletarians, Soviet philosophers submitted without protest to the dictates of the Communist Party, blindly following the indisputable party principle in the belief that the doctrines and concepts of the Communist Party reflected the fundamental interests and outlook of the revolutionary working class. Moreover, the myth of the invincibility of the party principle was carried to an extreme when Soviet philosophers claimed that, according to the doctrine of Marxism-Leninism, "strict objectivity and scientific rigor are combined with partisanship."[23] Apparently, Soviet theoreticians were oblivious to the logical inconsistency in their attempt to reconcile "objectivity," "scientific rigor," and "partisanship."

Even after Stalin's death, in the years of the "thaw," the party principle retained its authoritative influence in Soviet philosophy, not giving rise to dissatisfaction or criticism. On the contrary, after the period of relaxation, which lasted into the mid-1960s, the Leninist principle of partisanship in philosophy was praised in the resolutions of Party Congresses, as well as in editorials of the Soviet philosophical journal *Voprosy filosofii*. In a message to the editors of the philosophical journal, the Presidium of the Academy of Sciences of the USSR declared that one of the major tasks in philosophical work is the "intense propagation of Marxist-Leninist theories, and the promotion of achievements in the social sciences in the light of the Leninist tradition."[24]

It is also of particular interest that the Communist Party regularly issued directives reprinted faithfully in the philosophical journal. The party told the philosophers to concern themselves with specific problems connected with the concrete tasks of the "construction of communism." Only a close collaboration between the philosophers and the party would lead to the creation of a genuine Marxist-Leninist science.[25] A number of variations on this theme were given prominent display in *Voprosy filosofii* for most of its 1976 editions in the wake of the twenty-fifth Congress of the CPSU.

However, some recent Western studies of Soviet philosophy regarded the symptoms of tolerance toward divergent opinions in Soviet intellectual circles—especially in the mid-1960s—as evidence of a nascent change in the style of philosophical discourse. A survey of major publications in Soviet philosophy before the advent of *glasnost* shows that despite most of its rigid and preordained patterns, there were distinctive signs of serious change attributable to the somewhat more tolerant intellectual climate of the late 1950s and the mid-1960s. There was evidence of sharp and searching discussions in the areas of philosophy of science, philosophy of logic, and the history of philosophy. The principles and the laws of the dialectic and the categories of matter, development, motion, essence, form, and so forth, were subjected to a thorough reexamination. On the whole, however, it was too early to speak of a Soviet philosophy "awakened from dogmatic slumbers."[26] Soviet philosophers, true to the Leninist tradition, "upheld the purity and creative development of Marxist theory, organically combined their theoretical work with revolutionary practice, consistently pursued and developed the principles of proletarian internationalism, *implementing the principle of commitment to ideology*, and proceeded from the philosophical principles of dialectical and historical materialism."[27]

Obviously, Soviet philosophers treated the central ideas of Marxism-Leninism as fixed principles. Accordingly, in Soviet philosophy these ideas and principles were handled with a reverent philosophical passivity, as absolute universals that "incorporated the 'quintessence' of our historical epoch, namely—Marxism-Leninism."[28] This attitude of philosophical passivity in Soviet thought was, in many respects, very much the same as a case of arrested intellectual development and was richly compensated by a strong ideological posture dedicated to the "irreconcilable struggle between the socialist and bourgeois world outlook."[29] As I wrote in 1981, in this struggle, in which "pure" philosophy, cleared of its ideological counterweight, was the real loser, a blind commitment to any

> ideology constitutes a predicament more treacherous than the susceptibility of man to the vagaries of personal prejudice. If philosophers can admonish each other in matters of personal prejudice—how could they recognize and correct a pervasive bias (in our case Marxist-Leninist ideology) which all Soviet philosophers share[d] and conform[ed] to?[30]

With the mode of Soviet thought totally subordinated to ideology, the Soviet philosopher—his intellectual development guided by ground rules that discouraged any deviation from the official political views of the Communist Party—in questions of controversy, foreclosed the matter with a ready quotation from the Marxist-Leninist classics, in all probability unaware that it was not sound philosophical practice to cite one side without acknowledging the other. As a matter of fact, Soviet philosophers proclaimed an unquestioning faith in the statements of the "classic" authors of Marxism-Leninism, treating them with the least possible amount of critical interpretation.

Dialectical materialism, with all its ups and downs in the history of Soviet philosophy, provided the only plausible explanation for the revolution and the establishment of the Soviet political system. The dialectic emphasized the primacy of matter over consciousness, and in the practical realm it furnished the Soviet philosopher with a kind of narrow concentration for approaching and defining problems. Without the principles of Marxism-Leninism, with its dialectical tightrope acts of self-deception, much of Soviet reality became unintelligible. This is why most "liberal" (for lack of a better word) discussions in Soviet philosophical works did not dare to question the basic ideas and the significance of Marxism-Leninism as an instrument of social and ideological conservation. It is also possible that this was one of the reasons why the Soviet Union never produced a really outstanding philosopher.

Still, judging from its historical development, Marxism-Leninism was flexible in some respects. True, its basic formulations were virtually enshrined and Soviet philosophers never failed to pay homage to Marxist-Leninist ideals, even if they departed widely from the notions under discussion; nevertheless, some elements of the doctrine seemed to be more flexible and changed as circumstances demanded. The change took place after a long period of careful reexamination, in which Marxist-Leninist theory was forcefully adjusted to new facts and situations. Not surprisingly, even the newly formulated concepts or principles were presented as clear, logical conclusions, arrived at on the basis of the Leninist philosophical tradition.[31] On the whole, however, the basic premises and presuppositions of Soviet thought were absolutist and dogmatic (despite its claim that Marxism-Leninism was incompatible with dogmatism),[32] faithfully reflecting the coarse stereotype of official ideological norms. And even if some significant changes took place, one should not mistake those changes for symptoms of ideological regression. It was generally recognized that Marxist-Leninist tactics may have changed, but the ideological framework usually remained the same.

Some philosophical schools prosper, while others are long forgotten or neglected. They all succeed or fail in their attempts to provide an adequate and comprehensive explanation of reality on the basis of human reason and experience. The philosophical school that is capable of independent, clear, constructive thinking and has the courage to test its own theories by facts and analysis, without resorting to authority, has the best chance for long-lasting durability.

A philosophical school such as Marxism-Leninism lasted for a long time thanks to the powerful support of the former Soviet state. Nonetheless, it was this strong support that really harmed Soviet philosophy, because it exacted a high ideological price. In the absence of a genuine philosophical skepticism, and disdainful of the autonomy of inquiry, Soviet philosophy rested on a fixed particularism as its point of reference. As a result, Soviet philosophers, with a marked hostility to other ways of thinking, clung to their ideological faith, predetermined by Marxist-Leninist principles, without realizing that dogmatism is simply incompatible with reason. Moreover, the more elaborate the ideological framework, the less significant a philosopher's point becomes—indeed, Soviet philosophers, in praise of conformity above honesty, displayed a remarkable penchant for classifying and generalizing but were much less inclined to analyze critically sensitive political and philosophical issues.[33]

It is true that the quality and methods of philosophical inquiry in the former Soviet Union lost to a considerable degree the drabness and sterility so markedly prevalent during the Stalinist era. There were some professional practitioners of philosophy who, in the late 1950s and mid-1960s, made significant and sometimes daring contributions that might be of interest to their Western colleagues.[34] There was a noticeable shift of interest in the philosophy of science (especially among the younger generation of Soviet philosophers), with a concern for logic and the precision of language in sharp contrast to the speculative metaphysics of Marxism-Leninism. A small group of philosophers (represented most vocally by G. Batishchev, P. Egides, and L. Naumenko) even tried to develop interesting alternatives in reexamining the officially accepted reflection theory of knowledge.[35]

Still, the critical and expositive value of these philosophical works, as well as the levels of academic expertise, were mostly typical of the Soviet experience, in which allegiance to a singular, doctrinaire world outlook considerably narrowed the general perspectives of scholarly research and inquiry,[36] and which only served to confirm the late John Plamenatz's assertion that when we turn "from German to Russian Marxism, we leave the horses and come to the mules."[37]

Notes

1. M. Rosenthal and P. Yudin, eds., *A Dictionary of Philosophy* (Moscow: Progress Publishers, 1967), 34

2. *Fundamentals of Marxism-Leninism* (Moscow: Foreign Languages Publishing House, 1963), 46.

3. Cited in Gustav A. Wetter, *Dialectical Materialism* (New York: Frederick A. Praeger, 1963), 138.

4. Deborin is also known for being instrumental in publishing works of Western materialist philosophers.

5. Cited in Wetter, *Dialectical Materialism*, 160–61.

6. The word *kulak*—in its literal meaning, "a fist"—was used in the Marxist-Leninist lexicon as a derogatory label applied to well-off, more successful peasants.

7. Interestingly enough, Deborin survived the purges and remained in

Moscow until his death, occasionally contributing essays on noncontroversial subjects in the 1950s.

8. Cited in Wetter, *Dialectical Materialism*, 177.

9. M. B. Mitin, *Problemy sovremennoi ideologicheskoi borby* (Problems in the Contemporary Ideological Struggle) (Moscow, 1976), 61. On pages 9 and 10 Mitin also presented a spirited defense of the Leninist "party principle" in philosophy.

10. *An End to Silence*, ed. Stephen F. Cohen (New York: W. W. Norton & Co., 1982), 124–32.

11. Cited in Wetter, *Dialectical Materialism*, 183.

12. For a more extensive discussion of this period, see Werner G. Hahn, *Postwar Soviet Politics: The Fall of Zhdanov and the Defeat of Moderation, 1946–53* (Ithaca, N.Y.: Cornell University Press, 1982).

13. Cited in Wetter, *Dialectical Materialism*, 189.

14. "Dialectical logic is the logical teaching of dialectical materialism, science and the laws and forms of mental reflection of the development and change of the objective world, and of the laws governing the cognition of truth." (Rosenthal and Yudin, eds., *Dictionary of Philosophy*, 248). This is one of the many vague and obscure definitions of dialectical logic. It is really a pseudologic which can be neither verified nor refuted by means of the methodology of empirical sciences. See Ernst Topitsch, "How Enlightened is Dialectical Reason," *Encounter* (May 1982): 45–55.

15. *The Fundamentals of Marxist-Leninist Philosophy* (Moscow: Progress Publishers, 1974), 102. Henceforth referred to as *The Fundamentals*.

16. Ibid., 306.

17. Ibid., 315.

18. Ibid., 305.

19. Ibid., 327.

20. "The dialectical method regards as important primarily not that which at the given moment seems to be durable and yet is already beginning to die away, but that which is arising and developing, even though at the given moment it may appear not to be durable, for the dialectical method considers invincible only that which is arising and developing." J. V. Stalin, "O dialekticheskom i istoricheskom materializme," in *Voprosy Leninisma*, 11th ed. (Moscow, 1947), 535–63. ["On Dialectical and Historical Materialism," in *Problems of Leninism*].

21. For example, A. Chknaveriantz, *Kategorii Materialisticheskoi Dialektiki* (The Categories of Dialectical Materialism) (Moscow, 1966). Two hundred thousand copies of this pocket-size booklet (only fifty pages) were published.

22. M. Iovchuk, *Philosophical Traditions Today* (Moscow: Progress Publishers, 1973), 65.

23. The *Fundamentals*, 660.

24. *Voprosy filosofii*, no. 5 (1969): 145. Also in no. 4 (1980): 14.

25. *Voprosy filosofii*, no. 4 (1971): 12.

26. *Philosophy in the Soviet Union: A Survey of the Mid-Sixties*, ed. Erwin Laszlo (Sovietica, New York: Praeger, 1967), v.

27. Iovchuk, *Philosophical Traditions Today*, 143. Emphasis added.
28. Ibid., 294.
29. Ibid., 294.
30. Sigmund Krancberg, "The Science of Logic in Soviet Philosophy and a Reading in Hegelian Dialectics," *Studies in Soviet Thought* 22 (1981): 93.
31. Iovchuk, *Philosophical Traditions Today*, 298-99.
32. *The Fundamentals*, 661.
33. For a good introduction to Soviet philosophy, see Richard T. De George, *Patterns of Soviet Thought* (Ann Arbor: University of Michigan Press, 1966).
34. K. S. Bakradze, *Sistema i metod filosofii Gegelya* (System and Method in Hegel's Philosophy) (Tbilisi, 1958). This is one of the few Soviet philosophical works which deserves an English translation.
35. According to *The New York Times*, October 22, 1977, A-9, P. Egides lost his teaching job and joined the growing ranks of Soviet dissidents.
36. A somewhat altered version of this chapter appeared as Sigmund Krancberg, "Soviet Philosophy," *Survey* 28, no. 3 (Autumn 1984): 157-72, © *Survey*. (*Survey* magazine ceased publication in June, 1989).
37. John Plamenatz, *German Marxism and Russian Communism* (New York and London: Longmans, Green & Co., 1954) 191.

6

The Profile of an Empire: The World Socialist System

> Whoever occupies a territory also imposes on it his own social system. Everyone imposes his own system as far as his army can reach. It cannot be otherwise.
>
> J. V. Stalin[1]

A curious mixture of doctrine, theory, and dogma which by its very nature defies empirical scrutiny, is the most conspicuous feature of Soviet political writings, from scholarly Marxist-Leninist studies of the "dialectic" to the coarse style of the 1961 *Programme of the Soviet Communist Party*.[2]

Proclaiming "the historical necessity of the transition from capitalism to socialism," the authors of the *Programme of the Soviet Communist Party* emphasized that "the Soviet Union does not pursue the tasks of Communist construction alone but in fraternal community with the other socialist countries."[3] Thus, the states once formally belonging to the former Soviet bloc—Bulgaria, Czechoslovakia, the Democratic Republic of Vietnam, the German Democratic Republic, Hungary, the Korean People's Democratic Republic, Poland, Rumania, Cuba, and the Mongolian People's Republic—represented what Soviet theoreticians characterized as the world socialist system.

According to the *Great Soviet Encyclopedia*, the world socialist system was "a social, economic, and political community of free sovereign states developing toward socialism and Communism and united by common interests and goals and by the bonds of international socialist solidarity."[4] Understandably, the *Great Soviet Encyclopedia* failed to mention the fact that thirty-two Soviet divisions stationed in the four European states closest to the West[5] served until 1989 as an effective restraint on the hesitant and sporadic attempts of some Communist Party rulers to liberalize domestic conditions.

Since the Marxist-Leninist ideology was one of the most signifi-

129

cant factors in the Soviet-East European relationship, it seems that from a purely realistic political perspective, this definition of the "socialist commonwealth" (*socialisticeskoe sodruzestvo*) suffered from a number of serious flaws.

The first problem was that the term "socialist" had originally been applied to some form of democracy and is still used accordingly in the political lexicon of the social-democratic movements of Western Europe.[6] In contrast, it was widely acknowledged that, when the term "socialist" was used by the Soviet Communists as a self-characterization, it was done in order to attribute democracy to Communist regimes.

Second, this definition of the world socialist system overlooked the preeminent position of the Soviet Union in Eastern Europe, where it exercised considerable influence and power over the domestic and foreign policies of the People's Democracies, which, despite their "sovereignty," appropriately retained only a low degree of political autonomy.

Moreover, the description of a community of nations supposedly "advancing along the paths of socialism and Communism"[7] not only confused the distant future with a rather shabby present but also pointed to the fact that the exercise of "socialist" power could not be viewed independently of ideology. With a substantial reduction in the methods of coercion after Stalin's death, this Marxist-Leninist ideology became an important cohesive force—a prime mover and guide to organized, purposeful action. Thus, with the principles of Marxist-Leninist ideology restricting the perimeters of social activity within the structural framework of the world socialist system, reality—at least political reality—became a coordinated reproduction of the official ideology and its inherent myths, which increasingly replaced rational beliefs as a source of meaningful political insights. The doctrinal and prescriptive value of ideological presuppositions was clearly expressed in the Soviet "scientific theory of development," which, in effect, asserted that "the formation of ideology, corresponding to the new [socialist] mode of production, has a considerable part to play in its triumph and consolidation."[8]

Undoubtedly reflecting the hazards of ideological presuppositions and their questionable reliability, the *Programme* stated:

> The objective laws of the world socialist system, the growth of productive forces of socialist society and the vital interests of the peoples of the socialist countries predetermine the increasing affinity of the various national economies. As Lenin foresaw, tendencies develop to-

wards the future creation of a world Communist economy according to one single plan.⁹

Ignoring the fact that no Communist revolutions had ever taken place according to the classical Marxist model, Soviet writers, following the canons of the party, acclaimed the birth of the "socialist commonwealth" as a "necessary stage in the world-revolutionary process"—a stage which represented "the prototype of the future social organization of all mankind."¹⁰

However, the question of whether ideological presuppositions are an adequate reflection of the world as it *ought* to be is not decided in wishful, quasi-prophetic statements, which can hardly be applied to the world as we know it. Returning to the more prosaic, unembellished recent past, Soviet writers spoke in glowing terms of the socialist community, united not only by the same type of political system and social ownership of the means of production but also by common interests, goals, and close ties of international socialist solidarity.

This socialist solidarity, interchangeable at times with the "principles of internationalism," served as a euphemism for the political control of the Soviet Union over Eastern Europe. As a rule, Soviet writers rarely spoke about the supremacy of the Soviet Union within the world socialist system. However, they never failed to stress the fact that the Communist Party of the Soviet Union had been and remained the universally recognized vanguard of the world Communist movement. Recalling the lessons of Hungary and Czechoslovakia, Soviet writers argued that a socialist country is responsible not only to its people but also to all socialist countries.

In the spirit of the *Pravda* article of September 25, 1968, published to justify the invasion of Czechoslovakia,¹¹ Soviet writers claimed that the member states of the world socialist system could not exercise their sovereignty in a manner indicating opposition to the interests of the socialist community. In other words, socialist unity was not a purely abstract, theoretical concept. Accordingly, the Soviet writer S. Sanakoyev wrote that socialist unity "presupposes definite action which follows from Marxist-Leninist ideology, from the principles of socialist internationalism, and which includes the common defense of the revolutionary gains of the peoples of every socialist country."¹² This was, in essence, the Brezhnev doctrine—proclaimed by Andrei Gromyko in his speech to the United Nations on October 3, 1968—which was a serious warning against any attempt to reform the political and ideological status quo in the People's Democracies.¹³ Hence it becomes clear that this demand for joint action to defend the "socialist commonwealth" also meant that the Brezhnev doctrine strongly denied the member states of the world socialist system any reliance on the international legal concept of self-determination and thus deprived them of the role of autonomous political actors.

However, contrary to the fact that the basic features of Soviet political supremacy in Eastern Europe remained relatively constant since Stalin's death, Soviet relations with the People's Democracies underwent a substantial change. When the Soviet Union refrained from issuing detailed instructions to its socialist allies on matters of domestic as well as foreign policy issues, the relationship between the USSR and the People's Democracies gradually changed from one where the latter assumed a purely subordinate character to an approximation of frequently strained but publicly "friendly" cooperation. Obviously, the ultimate question of Soviet political and ideological authority was hardly apparent in the much-touted treaties of friendship, alliance, and mutual assistance—treaties supposedly designed to further "the fraternal friendship between the peoples of socialist states . . . safeguarding their security and economic and political independence."[14]

Still, Soviet writers were reluctant to discuss the considerable changes that took place in the post-Stalin era. Certainly, they spoke in most general terms about the personality cult and the elimination of its consequences, but they hardly touched upon the process of de-Stalinization and the "thaw" that lasted from the mid-fifties to the mid-sixties. Curiously, Soviet writers somehow managed to discuss the various stages of development in the world socialist system without mentioning Stalin's or Khrushchev's name even once. It is a fact that, with Khrushchev's rise to power, a number of domestic reforms eliminated some of the most oppressive measures of the Stalinist era—reforms that were also aimed at correcting the most glaring excesses of centralized decision making.

Silent about Stalin's draconian policies in Eastern Europe—which went as far as the selection and removal of leaders through bloody purges in People's Democracies—Soviet writers extolled the "strong alliance" and the "unbreakable friendship" between the Soviet Union and the countries of the socialist commonwealth, which were legally consolidated into the socialist world system at the end of the 1940s.[15]

Interestingly enough, Soviet writers reserved the greatest enthusiasm for the founding of the Council for Mutual Economic Assistance (CMEA), which took place at a meeting held in Moscow in January, 1949. Proclaiming this meeting an event of primary historical importance for the further improvement of economic cooperation among the member countries of the world socialist system, Salva Sanakoyev, for example, spoke at length of Soviet economic assistance to the People's Democracies but mentioned only in passing the question of reparations paid by those countries that fought as allies of the Axis powers. According to Sanakoyev, "reparations paid by Rumania, Hungary, and other allies of Nazi Germany were nowhere near as onerous as they were after the First World War"[16]—a spurious statement to say the least, in view of the fact that the former Soviet Union, in the first years after the Second World War, was able to confiscate huge quantities of industrial equipment, worth several billion dollars, as reparations from countries that were in an equal state of ruin and devastation.

Moreover, the former Soviet Union used its military and political leverage to extract more than favorable concessions from such allied countries as Poland and Czechoslovakia. Poland was forced to sell its coal at a fraction of the world price, while in Czechoslovakia, the Soviet Union actually took possession and thoroughly exploited one of the richest uranium deposits in the world.

Another episode entirely ignored by Soviet writers was the establishment of joint stock companies in Eastern Europe. It is a matter of record that the Soviet government, while sharing the profits, hardly contributed anything at all to these joint stock companies. Instead, it simply stopped shipping some of the assets earmarked for reparations to the Soviet Union and diverted these claimed assets as the Soviet government's capital contribution to the jointly organized stock companies.

However, within a few years after Stalin's death—since the Soviet Union accepted (at least officially) the idea of separate paths to socialism and attempted with this changed attitude to create in Eastern Europe an atmosphere more conducive to mutual understanding and cooperation—in this new departure, the joint stock companies were disbanded. This event marked the beginning of the elimination of the most exploitative economic policies originated under Stalin's reign. Nevertheless, despite the increased, active cooperation among the members of CMEA—especially after the adoption of a formal charter in 1960—the Soviet Union succeeded in reorienting most of the economic activity in the People's Democracies (with the exception of Rumania) toward the East. Thus the Soviet Union continued to maintain its dominant position in coordinating the national economic plans of the member countries, while being careful not to enforce operational conformity. Taking into consideration the principles of interestedness and unanimity in Article 4 of the CMEA charter,[17] such enforced conformity would probably have had little chance of success.

Even Sanakoyev noted that Article 4 of the CMEA charter was a "crystalized principle" and that "this international organization [CMEA] operated on the basis of equality of all members, insuring respect for sovereignty and national interests, mutual benefits and comradely assistance,"[18] knowing full well that even if a member country were forced to adopt a CMEA recommendation on a given project, the member country could have chosen an ineffective implementation of this undertaking.

However, this equality of status guaranteed by the charter of the CMEA was more imaginary than real. As Giovanni Graziani points out, the diversity of ways and means at the levels of economic activity of the CMEA members assured the Soviet Union—as a large country "with many resources and a high level industrialization"[19]—a controlling, hegemonic position while it relegated the lesser countries of the CMEA to mere dependencies. What Graziani failed to realize, in spite of the fact that he touched upon the problem of oil and energy imports from the Soviet Union, was that in a way the member states of CMEA exploited the Soviet Union in the pricing relationship of petroleum deliveries. Not only did the People's Democracies pay prices somewhat lower than non-Communist buyers, but the transactions were based not on hard currency but on bartering goods in exchange for the lower-priced Soviet petroleum. (At present, this relationship is a matter of the past and former members of CMEA experience serious energy problems.) It seems that this was the price the former Soviet Union had to pay for maintaining an empire.

Not surprisingly, statements concerning political stability and "socialist integration" were typical of the official reports on CMEA activities. Such statements were the expression of policies that reaffirmed close economic cooperation while vaguely implying promises of mutual rewards. For example, a *Survey of CMEA Activities*, published by its Secretariat in Moscow, stated that the CMEA member countries continued to "implement consistently the strategic course of the communist and Workers' Parties towards the intensification of social production, the acceleration of scientific and technical progress, and the extension of economic cooperation among the CMEA member countries."[20] It is noteworthy that the *Survey* never mentioned the low living standards in CMEA countries—apparently an irreversible economic liability.

However, the *Survey* listed, in a very general manner, a number of fields of cooperation (planning, science, technology, energy, raw materials, etc.), including a terse report regarding a meeting of the Political Consultative Committee of Warsaw Treaty member states held in Prague on an unspecified date. The purpose of the meeting was stated as "consistently countering the military course of imperialism, halting the arms race and safeguarding peace."[21]

Similarly, calling for greater socialist cooperation and international solidarity, the thirty-sixth Meeting of the Session of the Council for Mutual Economic Assistance, held in Budapest in June, 1982, was chiefly attended by the prime ministers of the CMEA member states, including General W. Jaruzelski. The meeting took notice of the "complicated" international situation, which was a result of the "intensified policy pursued 'from strength' by the imperialist powers, with their increased military spending and interference in the internal affairs of other countries."[22] Consequently, in connection with the American sanctions and the curtailment of trade and economic ties to Poland, the meeting acknowledged this "inadmissible" interference in the internal affairs of the Polish People's Republic, assuring the fraternal Polish people of continued support in overcoming their economic difficulties (political difficulties were ignored), and guaranteeing the creation of conditions "for further socialist development of the country."[23]

But urgent calls from Moscow for greater socialist cooperation and international solidarity failed "to win the acknowledgment of the populations that the [Communist] regimes had a right to rule."[24] What the Council for Mutual Economic Assistance did not take into account, was that the 1980–1981 political crisis in Poland underscored the pressures for change in the climate of a progressive deformation of socialism. Moreover, huge foreign debts, economic hardships, the gradual loss of political authority, and lack of support from the Soviet Union[25] marked the beginning of the de-satellization[26] process, which culminated in the peaceful disintegration (with the exception of Rumania) of the world socialist system in 1989, followed by the dismantling of the Council for Mutual Economic Assistance and the Warsaw Pact.

It is a fact that the developments in Eastern Europe between 1980 and 1989, which led to the demise of communism in the region, cannot be explained in terms of the Marxist theory of revolution. The historical events in Eastern Europe did not take place as a result of the "class struggle" or because of glaring contradictions between the forces of production and the relations of production. Apparently, the East European peoples' demand for justice, democracy, truth, legality, human dignity, and freedom of convictions proved much stronger than Stalin's dictum, which was perpetuated in spirit as well as in deed by the Brezhnev doctrine: "Whoever occupies a territory also imposes on it his own social system. Everyone imposes his system as far as his army can reach."

Notes

1. J. V. Stalin, in Milovan Djilas, *Conversations with Stalin* (New York: Harcourt, Brace and World, 1962), 114.

2. Chapter Six appeared as Sigmund Krancberg, "The Socialist World System: Alliance or Instrument of Domination?" *Studies in Soviet Thought* 30 (1985): 55-63, © 1985 by D. Reidel Publishing Company; reprinted here by permission of Kluwer Academic Publishers.

3. *Programme of the Communist Party of the Soviet Union* (Moscow: Foreign Languages Publishing House, 1961), 12.

4. *Great Soviet Encyclopedia,* vol. 16 (New York: Macmillan, 1977), 679.

5. *Current History* (April, 1978): 145.

6. In the words of *The Oxford Universal Dictionary*, socialism is "the ownership and control of the means of production by the community as a whole, and their administration or distribution in *the interests of all*" (emphasis added).

7. Salva Sanakoyev, *The World Socialist System* (Moscow: Progress Publishers, 1975), 104; *Dictionary of Philosophy*, ed. M. Rosenthal and P. Yudin (Moscow: Progress Publishers, 1967), 483.

8. G. P. Frantsov, *Philosophy and Sociology* (Moscow: Progress Publishers, 1975), 392.

9. Cited in Sanakoyev, *World Socialist System*, 106.

10. G. P. Frantsov, *Philosophy and Sociology*, 409, and Sanakoyev, *World Socialist System*, 105.

11. Reprinted in the translation of the Soviet Press Agency in *New York Times*, September 27, 1968, 3.

12. Sanakoyev, *World Socialist System*, 269.

13. Cited in Thomas M. Frank and Edward Weisband, *World Politics* (New York and London: Oxford University Press, 1972), 34–35.

14. Sanakoyev, *World Socialist System*, 42.

15. A. A. Gromyko and B. N. Ponomarev, eds., *Soviet Foreign Policy,* 4th ed., vol. 2 (Moscow: Progress Publishers, 1980), 57.

16. Sanakoyev, *World Socialist System*, 42.

17. Article 4 of the CMEA charter states: "All recommendations and decisions by the Council shall be adopted only with the consent of the interested member countries of the Council, and each country shall be entitled to declare its interest in any matter considered by the Council. The effects of recommendations and decisions shall not extend to countries which have declared their lack of interest in the question concerned" (cited in Michael Kaser, *Comecon: Integration Problems of the Planned Economies* [New York and London: Oxford University Press, 1967], 238).

18. Sanakoyev, *World Socialist System*, 229.

19. Giovanni Graziani, "Dependency Structure in Comecon," *The Review of Radical Political Economics* 13, no. 1 (Spring 1981): 71.

20. *Survey of CMEA Activities between the 36th and 37th Meetings of the Session of the Council* (Moscow, 1983), 3.

21. Ibid., 8.

22. Ibid., 64.

23. Ibid. The *Survey* provided no hard statistical data, merely growth indicators in percentage points.

24. Zwi Gitelman, "The Roots of Eastern Europe's Revolution," *Problems of Communism* (May-June, 1990): 89.

25. Mikhail Gorbachev removed the threat of Soviet intervention when he stated in October 1989 in Finland: "We have no right, moral or political right, to interfere in events happening there" (*New York Times*, October 26, 1989). Needless to say, this statement signaled the end of the Brezhnev doctrine.

26. Ernst Kux, "Revolution in Eastern Europe—Revolution in the West?" *Problems of Communism* (May-June, 1991): 3. Also cited in *Kommunist*, 1 (January, 1990): 105.

7

Conclusion:
The Disintegration of the Soviet Union and the Journey into the Unknown

> In building the so-called *radiant future*, we have been to hell and back, as they say. . . . But we have still had the strength to stop, and then begin the process of a most difficult ascent to normal life.[1]
>
> Boris Yeltsin
>
> Uncertainty as to what the future has in store casts its heavy and black shadow over all aspects of the present.[2]
>
> John Dewey

After the overthrow of the czar in 1917, Alexander Kerensky, the head of the Provisional Government, lamented:

> The word "revolution" is quite inapplicable to what happened in Russia (in February 1917). A whole world of national and political relationships sank to the bottom, and at once all existing political and tactical programs, however bold and well conceived, appeared hanging aimlessly in space.[3]

What Kerensky neglected to state in his lament was the fact that czarist Russia did not prepare for the end but resisted it until the abdication of Nicholas II—an event that highlighted the demise of the tsarist empire in a last gasp of the three-hundred-year-old Romanov dynasty. With the collapse of the monarchy and the empire, "power lay in the streets for eight months before the Bolsheviks picked it up."[4] And it was mainly because of this lack of preparation for a major breakdown of czarist rule that the 1917 February Revolution generated political confusion, marked by alarming symptoms of anarchy—a set of circumstances that contributed greatly to the failure to create a social order based on a methodical and gradual transition to democracy.

The Bolshevik seizure of power was likewise far from an orderly and rationally managed affair. In their aversion to the principle of humanizing conduct—a conduct committed to a peaceful resolution of conflicting interests—the Bolshevik elite ignored the major requirements of responsible political thought and practice observed in any brand of civilized politics. Determined to settle matters according to their interpretation of socialist doctrine, the Bolsheviks, overstepping the limits of our human condition, established a totalitarian state with a loyal political infrastructure built on sheer might, will, and brutal power.[5] Moreover, the virtually canonized principle commonly known in Marxist parlance as "the unity of theory and practice" worked itself into an unprincipled praxis, manifested in a convulsive, savage activism that mindlessly sacrificed the lives of millions of people in the name of a distant, utopian goal. As Giovanni Sartori noted: "It is by now abundantly clear that there is no innate creativity in revolutionary violence. In and of itself, collective violence simply destroys."[6]

The degeneration of the Bolshevik dictatorship into "a power that is not limited by any laws, not bound by any rules, and is based directly on force"[7] compromised and impoverished the Communist ideas and plans for social development as an ordered and continuous process of social growth. In the long run, with the lack of legal safeguards against the abuse of power, the sordid reality of Soviet social and political life contributed to the fragility and collapse of the Soviet system—a system that originated "in a utopia that led to its practical failure."[8] Thus, from a practical political viewpoint, Bolshevism—in a massive attempt to substitute ideology for reality[9]—lost in the course of its history the political, moral, and intellectual standing in the countless inhuman excesses of War Communism and forced collectivization, in the extensive purges and Moscow trials, in the Hitler-Stalin pact, and in the autocratic, cruel, and oppressive treatment of the Soviet people after the Second World War. And all these atrocities were committed in the name of a Marxist-Leninist ideology that considered violence as the midwife of history.

Despite its severe limitations, Khrushchev's secret speech at the closed session of the Twentieth Party Congress in February 1956 had a tremendous impact on the Communist regime. Even if the secret speech was limited to the exposure of Stalin's crimes only against the party elite—without mentioning the millions of innocent, ordinary Soviet people who perished in prisons and concentration camps—Khrushchev, in denouncing the "cult of personality," succeeded in proving that the history of the Soviet Communist Party under Stalin's leadership consisted of criminal acts and mass murder—crimes that turned the principle of "socialist legality" into a mockery.

But the short-lived "thaw" in the wake of Khrushchev's secret speech was doomed to failure from the beginning. Only a few months after the secret speech, the Stalinist hard-liners began an offensive against Khrushchev which led to a resolution adapted by the CPSU Central Committee in which Stalin was hailed as a great leader and as an "extraordinary theoretician and organizer." In the resolution, Stalin was also given credit not only for his successful struggle against the opposition but also for assuring "the victory of socialism" in the Soviet Union and for developing "the Communist and national liberation movements around the world."[10]

Khrushchev's second attempt to revive the de-Stalinization campaign in 1961 echoed the new party line denouncing Stalin's cult of personality and is best remembered for the publication of Alexander Solzhenitsyn's novel *One Day in the Life of Ivan Denisovich*, a masterful chronicle depicting the flagrant, widespread abuses of "socialist legality." (Solzhenitsyn's other works, *The First Circle, Cancer Ward*, and *The Gulag Archipelago* appeared only in the West.)

It is noteworthy that Khrushchev, after his forced retirement, declared in his memoir, *Khrushchev Remembers*: "Criminal acts had been committed by Stalin, acts which would be punishable in any state in the world except in fascist states like Hitler's and Mussolini's."[11] Critical commentators in the West had often compared fascist and Communist dictatorships in terms of totalitarian principles,[12] but this was indeed a rare occasion when a Soviet leader drew a comparison between a Communist and a fascist state structure.

Under Leonid Brezhnev, and during the short reign of the gerontocrats Yuri Andropov and Konstantin Chernenko, the overt condemnation of Stalin came to an end, while the official policy aimed at reinstating the prestige of the party was combined with a semi-covert campaign of re-Stalinization.[13] Regardless of the cumulative effects of economic stagnation, social corrosion, and widespread apathy, the Soviet Communist Party, bent on preserving its commanding position, directed an effort to develop organizational improvements of social control in a single-minded attempt to streamline the existing centralized system by implementing the well-publicized formula "scientific management of society" (see Chapter 4).[14] In the same spirit, Article 6 of the newly adapted Constitution of 1977 formalized the role of the party, defining it as "the leading and guiding force of Soviet society [which] directs the great constructive work of the Soviet people, and imparts a planned, systematic and theoretically substantiated character of their struggle for the victory of communism."[15]

True to form, almost two decades later—only a year after Mikhail Gorbachev was selected by the Politburo as secretary general—the new

Programme of the Communist Party of the Soviet Union, approved at the twenty-seventh Congress on March 1, 1986, reaffirmed the commanding position of the party, self-assuredly proclaiming to the world that "transition from capitalism to socialism and communism" represents "the main content of the present epoch."[16] If the 1961 Programme hailed the glorious revolutionary mission of the Soviet Union, declaring that *"the world capitalist system as a whole is ripe for a social revolution of the proletariat,"*[17] the new Programme, in a somewhat more subdued revolutionary mood, still asserted that we live in an epoch *"of historical competition between two world socio-political systems"* and that "the advance of humanity towards socialism and communism, despite all its unevenness, complexity and contradictoriness, *is inevitable.*"[18]

As expected, following the publication of the Programme of 1986, Soviet newspapers and periodicals carried countless editorials, developing general guidelines for Soviet theoreticians and the agit-prop apparatus, placing selectively great stress on unemployment, racial strife, and social malaise as the pervasive evils of the "doomed" capitalist system, regardless of the widening gap between Soviet and Western living standards.

By contrast, with the advent of the warming currents of *glasnost*, there was in existence a new trend—a trend that made its appearance in socio-political and historical literature—the proponents of which seemed determined to look differently at the West while slowly freeing themselves from the party-imposed stereotypes that demonized capitalism. Such proponents, most of them latter-day democrats, believed that Marxism-Leninism with its "dogmatic scholasticism" was "an obstacle and not an aid to the understanding of the modern world."[19] They were also convinced that, in contradiction of Marxist-Leninist tenets, the two systems—capitalism and socialism—should enter into a continuous dialogue with each other, that they must adapt to each other, "mutually enrich and compete with each other—not to the harm but to the benefit of the future."[20] This cautious evaluation of the two systems of developed socialism and capitalism may be explained as the first hesitant step in the early phase of *glasnost*.

Nonetheless, with the passage of time, the critique and contempt for the Soviet system expanded and deepened. As Professor Martin Malia observed:

> *Glasnost* was exploited by increasingly radical intellectuals to expose the crimes of the past and the evils of the present. This, together with growing awareness of the economic gap between Russia and the out-

side world, soon destroyed what was left of the myth that socialism was leading to a "radiant future."[21]

Still laboring under the illusion that the "achievements" of socialism were irreversible, the CPSU, at a conference in June, 1988, adapted a resolution with the promising title: "On the Democratization of Soviet Society and Reform of the Political System."[22] A careful reading of this long-winded resolution, supposedly signaling a move toward liberalization, shows that this party effort was designed to assure an expansion of Gorbachev's presidential powers while it made provisions to protect the vital interests of the Communist elite. Calling for the strengthening "by all possible means"[23] of the authority of the Communist leadership, the resolution also reflected the tension between the need for free individual expression and the need for a revival of the party. It was in this atmosphere of tension, which took place within the framework of conflicting social and political orientations, that Gorbachev's ideas of reformed communism dominated the Soviet countryside between 1985 and 1990—bringing freedoms unparalleled since 1917.

Building on Andropov's brief and largely ineffective efforts to reform the Soviet economy, and declaring war on the institutionalized inertia and the widespread corruption in economic relationships, Gorbachev initiated sweeping changes in the social, political, and economic life of the country. With *glasnost*[24] as a vital element of the "new strategic organization"[25]—a slogan invented by Soviet leaders—Gorbachev relaxed the restrictions of ideological state censorship, thus encouraging a free flow of information within society, opening the political process to new opposition groups while broadening the scope of legitimate political activity, as exemplified in the organization of the first semi-free elections to the Congress of People's Deputies in March, 1989. This legislative body was formally established in December, 1988, when the Supreme Soviet—formerly "the highest organ of state authority of the USSR"[26]—voted itself out of existence, creating in its place the Congress of People's Deputies, consisting of 2,250 members. It is noteworthy that these elections turned into an historical event which resulted in a massive ground swell of support for the creative intelligentsia, who offered programs of reform built on democratic principles.

At the same time, the growing recognition of the terrible inefficiencies of the Soviet system, with its social decay and the faltering command economy, was reflected in Gorbachev's catchword of *"perestroika"* (restructuring)—a shorthand designation for a major policy initiative that stood for a radical social, political, and economic reform. Hence, according to Gorbachev, the reforms had to encompass

> not only the economy but all other sides of social life: social relations, the political system, the spiritual and ideological sphere, the style and work methods of the Party and all our cadres. "Restructuring" is a capacious word. I would equate restructuring with revolution in the minds and hearts of the people.[27]

Despite its novelty and great significance, *perestroika* failed to alleviate the deepening economic crisis exacerbated by the tradition of rigid planning, poor growth in productivity, and lagging technological performance. To be sure, Gorbachev introduced six ambitious economic programs within two years (1989–1990), but these programs were never carried out because of indecision at the center, parliamentary wrangling, and bureaucratic red tape.

However, the political success of *perestroika* was clearly responsible for allowing unprecedented cultural freedoms, enhanced by Gorbachev's pledge to place human rights at "the center of everything."[28] Curiously, these "rights and freedoms lacked institutionalization"—an arrangement that is guaranteed by the legal system of a law-governed state.[29] Apparently, Gorbachev's speeches displayed a tension and ambiguity which were astutely defined by Peter Juviler: "He [Gorbachev] symbolized more than ever, within himself, the unresolved conflicts of transition from old Communist loyalties and values to new democratic commitments."[30]

It seems that, as the true son of a party that effectively prevented for the previous seventy years the introduction of democracy as a political alternative, Gorbachev—despite his commitment to the process of democratization—was, at bottom, a "within-system reformer" who "want[ed] to make the existing order successful by effecting changes in it."[31] Accordingly, Gorbachev affirmed on frequent occasions his allegiance to Lenin, emphasizing that it was important "to know how to act, as Lenin taught us, by virtue of authority, energy, greater experience, greater versatility, and greater talent."[32] Similarly, in his important speech on February 13, 1987—a speech unnoticed in the West—Gorbachev, addressing media and propaganda chiefs, compared the then-current situation of the Soviet Union "with that faced by Lenin in 1918 when he signed the disastrous Brest-Litovsk Treaty with Germany." Gorbachev went on to say that "as in 1918, the Revolution would recover and resume its forward march."[33]

Sharing with Lenin his hostility toward political pluralism, and unable or unwilling to discard the ideological jargon of Marxism-Leninism, Gorbachev presented in the fall of 1988 his revised conception of pluralist politics:

> When you regularly follow the papers and journals, you get the impression that certain authors and even organizations have already distributed themselves into certain papers and journals. Today I can tell you exactly which letters this journal will publish and which one that will. Group passions are appearing. And we must overcome this. Publish everything. There must be a pluralism of opinion. But with such an orientation that the line of *perestroika, the interests of socialism are defended and strengthened*."[34]

Interestingly enough, only a few months later, Gorbachev, addressing a group of industrial workers, "characterized the talk of a multiparty system as 'rubbish'."[35] And again, following the March 1989 elections that returned the party maverick Boris Yeltsin, Gorbachev declared that "we must not commit stupidities, attempt great leaps forward, or overreach ourselves because we could put the people's future at risk. At a practical level the creation of more political parties is not a solution."[36]

These clear pronouncements confirmed that Gorbachev was not a "fence-straddler" and that he was very active in supporting hardliners' efforts designed to preserve the leading role of the Communist Party in the "natural, original role as conceived by Lenin."[37] Accordingly, as late as December 1989, at the Second Congress of People's Deputies, Gorbachev tried to stop a debate on Article 6 of the Soviet Constitution—an attempt that was eventually defeated. Remarkably, a year later, the Central Committee of the Soviet Communist Party, at its February 5–7 Plenum, declared itself for honest elections open to "representatives of all strata of society," abandoning for the party any claim to a "special position."[38] But as Charles Fairbanks points out, a growing faction—perhaps a majority—in the party apparatus criticized Gorbachev's reform initiatives as threats to the party and the USSR. As Fairbanks indicates, this makes it all the more "astonishing" that only 2 of the 270 participants in the plenum opposed Gorbachev's proposal.[39]

The collapse of opposition within the party, however, reflected its inability to abandon the central political tenets of Leninism even in the interest of its own survival: the party followed its leader as democratic centralism "turned against itself" in what amounted to a kind of suicide.[40] Curiously, even after Article 6 was rescinded, *Pravda*, under the heading "What People Are Talking About—Who Can I Complain to Now?" published the following observation:

> One would have thought that the rescinding of Article Six of the Constitution, which codified the CPSU's leading role, and the separation of the Party, Soviet and economic functions should have facilitated the development of law-governed relations in society and the putting in order of our entire life. Unfortunately, so far this hasn't happened. . . . As a result, not only individuals but entire collectives and organizations have found themselves disarmed in the face of high-handed behavior of functionaries, bureaucrats and unscrupulous people. "Democracy" is turning into lawlessness and anarchy.[41]

In retrospect, it is reasonably obvious that, regardless of the strong movement dedicated to eliminating Article 6 from the constitution, Gorbachev—always inclined to go with the prevailing political winds—by the fall of 1990, was leaning strongly in the direction of the hardliners, appointing military representatives, KGB officials, and senior party apparatchiks to top government posts, declaring that the party "must, resolutely and without delay, restructure all its work and reorganize all its structures . . . so that under the new conditions it can effectively perform its role as the vanguard Party."[42]

Affected by the aftershocks of the collapse of Communist regimes in Eastern Europe in 1989, the hardliners—now in commanding government posts—accused the democrats of instigating anarchy and destabilization in an attempt to slow down the pace of transformation. Oblivious of the countless cases of massive civil disobedience—such as the refusal of provincial bureaucrats to follow orders from the center, the strikes in the coal basins of the country, the formation of paramilitary organizations in Armenia, and the huge rallies in Azerbaijan, just to name a few—the hardliners acted like chief "ideologists of the 'revolution from above' [with] unhurried thoroughness . . . but without thinking through the consequences."[43]

The original design of *perestroika* met the test of logic—but a logic that was poorly served by the continuously worsening economy. Still, the very different political game in progress unmistakably proved that coercion, suppression, and mindless conformism would no longer be of any help. Subjected to the hardships and deprivations of economic scarcity, accompanied by the return to power of the heavy-handed, conservative hardliners, the people experienced a strong feeling of uncertainty and a vague premonition of danger. According to one perceptive observer of the Soviet scene, this impending disaster could materialize in the form of two threats:

The first was the restoration of a totalitarian system through the joint efforts of fundamentalist Party apparatchiks, some of our generals, the State Security Committee, and the Russian nationalists who sided with them. The second was designated by public affairs writers as an "explosion," "civil war," "the Rumanian option," or "Lebanonization"—frightening terms that were not really well analyzed or precisely defined.[44]

The expectation of something unknown that might come about intensified with the buildup of economic chaos. The hardliners—heads of KGB, the MVD (the regular police), and the military—again lashed out against the reformist movement, promising to restore order while trying to prevent the disintegration of the Soviet state.

In February, 1991, overwhelmed by the formidable task of extricating the country from the deepening economic crisis, Gorbachev once more reaffirmed his commitment to democracy but declared at the same time that "I am a Communist and faithful to the idea of socialism. I will . . . go on to the next world with this. . . . That we serve within the framework of the Communist Party is an idea that unites and reflects the interests of all strata of our people."[45] However, only two months later, Gorbachev, in a theatrical gesture and without any explanation, offered his resignation at a Joint Plenary Session of the CPSU Central Committee and the CPSU Central Control Commission. During the ensuing discussion, Gorbachev's resignation was "removed from consideration,"[46] whereupon Gorbachev, reaffirming his Bolshevik credentials, stated:

> Serious- and sober-minded people will not let the Party be knocked off the path of reform. Its chance of rebirth as a vanguard political force[47] consists in doing everything it can to promote the renewal of our society in its chosen path. If this line prevails, the people will again support the Party, and it will have no fear of any political opponent. I am ready to go with this democratic, popular current to the end.[48]

Surprisingly, at the Plenum's end (April 27, 1991), Gorbachev suddenly remembered that Article 6 was no longer valid and, in his concluding speech, abandoned his infatuation with the leading role of the party, stating:

> The Party has deliberately given up the monopoly on power that it held for decades. I see that this is hitting people very hard, that it is difficult for everyone to accept. . . . Many new forces have entered the political arena. All this has utterly changed the political climate. We have to understand this and find our role, one that is fitting at this

new stage of development of our society. I repeat, this is hard for us. Nostalgia for the old ways has not left us Party officials.[49]

Although he brought upon himself the bitter enmity of top party bureaucrats, Gorbachev was still unbending in his support of the KGB. In May, 1991, the Supreme Soviet, under strong pressure from Gorbachev, enacted a bill charging the KGB with the task of fighting "economic crimes." Giving the KGB new, sweeping powers, including the legal right "to seize business documents and bank statements and to search the premises of private enterprises for evidence of sabotage,"[50] represented a turn of events that alarmed the reformers, who considered this bill a serious threat to democracy. Encouraged by the successful passage of this bill, "KGB Chairman Vladimir Kryuchkov [somewhat later one of the leaders of the coup] had been especially outspoken about the need to put brakes on reform."[51] Giving free rein to the KGB, Gorbachev refused to assume responsibility for the bloody attacks on the democratic governments of Lithuania and Latvia in January, June, and July, 1991.[52]

Nonetheless, Gorbachev's refusal to abandon *perestroika* and his insistence that the reforms must continue kept the conservative hardliners off balance. At the same time, transferring power to the state authorities, Gorbachev slowly reduced the prestige of the party apparatus. This weakening of the party and the gradual diffusion of power created a chaotic state of affairs that further antagonized the military top brass, the KGB, and the ideological watchdogs of the party. Alarmed by the leftward surge in the country, Gorbachev's conservative colleagues tried to prevent him from signing a new union treaty designed to preserve the unity of the state in the form of a loose confederation.

Rumors of an impending coup started at the end of 1990 and reemerged with greater intensity in the spring and early summer of 1991.[53] With rumors afloat, the hardliners expanded their attacks on the reformers in an attempt to ward off the disintegration of Soviet power. Marshal Sergey Akhromeyev, who committed suicide after the coup failed, "vigorously joined in the ugly attacks on Andrei Sakharov, weeks before the coup, [after] he barred publication of an anti-Stalinist study of Soviet readiness for World War II."[54] On July 23, 1991, the reactionary newspaper *Sovetskaya Rossiya* published a manifesto under the title "Word to the People" which amounted to an "open call for a coup against Gorbachev."[55]

Apparently, Gorbachev's minimal retreat from the reform agenda and his attempt to turn back toward traditional central controls to deal directly with the economic and political crisis did not appease the hardliners. On August 19, 1991, taking advantage of Gorbachev's absence—he was vacationing at his summer home in the sea resort in the Crimea—and citing the imminent dangers of the Union treaty, which would have transferred power from the center to the republics, the ringleaders of the coup (the heads of KGB, the MVD, and some top military officers, including the Minister of Defense) ousted Gorbachev from power. Placing Gorbachev, who was in good health, under house arrest in the Crimea and trying to justify their seizure of power, the plotters called attention to Gorbachev's inability, for reasons of ill health, to perform his duties as president. Announcing that all power in the country had been transferred to the newly formed State Emergency Committee, the leaders of the coup issued an "Appeal to the Soviet People" that condemned "extremist forces" bent on destroying the Soviet Union. After the "Appeal," the leader of the coup, Gennadiy Yanaev, the "faceless bureaucrat,"[56] (Gorbachev's vice-president, whom he trusted *completely*),[57] proclaimed that "our multi-ethnic people have lived for ages full of pride for their motherland" and assured the country that the State Emergency Committee had "a program of activities aimed at lowering the tensions that exist in the field of inter-ethnic relations."[58] As if trying to compensate for the vague and shallow content of their statements on the nationalities problem, the Committee demanded "that nationalist leaders be brought to account for the deaths of hundreds of victims of inter-ethnic conflicts," asserting that "the fate of more than half a million refugees" was "on their conscience."[59]

It is not at all surprising that, according to William E. Odom, director of National Security Studies for the Hudson Institute, Yeltsin's people "are discovering that camps in the Gulag were ready to receive prisoners, tribunals for summary trials were organized, and extensive lists of persons to be arrested had been compiled [by the leaders of the coup]."[60]

But the historical events during the three days that shook the world in August, 1991 were played out on the streets surrounding the Russian parliamentary building. Resistance to the coup increased as loyal throngs rallied to defend Yeltsin, who turned the Russian parliamentary building into a symbolic fortress against the plotters while displaying strength and eloquence under tremendous pressure. Despite the meager support from the working class of Moscow—according to a Soviet observer, "a significant part of the population in no way expressed its support for the democratic forces"[61]—Yeltsin's defiant stand, Gorbachev's refusal to cooperate with the coup leaders, and the vital support of key military commanders,[62] with their tank units protecting the Parliament building, doomed the ill-conceived plot to failure.

However, these were not the only reasons why the August coup failed. It is now a matter of historical record that the leaders of the coup bungled the takeover of the Soviet government because of the following missteps:

1. The leaders simply forgot to use the controversial "black beret" commandos, known as Omon—units formed by hardline Communists seeking to roll back the democratization process in the former Soviet Union.

2. The attempt to storm buildings with columns of tanks, although the coup leaders had at their disposal machine gun-equipped helicopters, is simply incomprehensible.

3. The plotters "placed Gorbachev and his family under house arrest and cut his telephone lines with the outside world. They left him, however, with a radio receiver capable of listening to foreign broadcasts, including the BBC World Service and the Voice of America!"[63]

4. The plotters allowed Yeltsin—who found himself at center stage—to use state television to call on the army to defy coup leaders.

5. Somehow, the coup leaders never interfered with Yeltsin's frequent telephone calls to the president of the United States and other world leaders.

These were the major oversights of the coup leaders, who probably assumed that the participation of the KGB and MVD heads was the best insurance that all preparations for the coup had been put in place. Actually, Victor Karpukhin, the commander of a KGB elite force, claimed that he had never received the order to storm the Russian Parliament.[64] Equally mysterious is the lack of preparation for Yeltsin's arrest—according to some sources, the KGB operatives entrusted with this task missed him by forty minutes.[65]

To summarize the collapse of the coup, it is clear that the ringleaders behaved like silly amateurs who displayed a hazy understanding of the ways and means to restore stability and order in the Soviet Union. In their desire to roll back history to 1985, and worried more about losing power and privilege, they so much "love[d] the old days *that they forgot their old ways!*"[66]

To be sure, there are doubts and questions about Gorbachev's role *before* the coup. Perhaps Gorbachev inadvertently encouraged the plotters in their undertaking, and perhaps they even expected him to participate in the State Emergency Committee. We have no answers to these conjectures, but it is a matter of fact that Gorbachev appeared worried about the forthcoming trials of the coup leaders who "might portray his role in a compromising light."[67]

In the wake of the August coup, the Soviet Union disintegrated into fifteen different republics. As Mark Beisinger observed: "The events of August merely furnished the setting in which that disintegration transpired, providing a cathartic end to an empire whose legitimating myth had long been punctured, whose institutions were crumbling, and which was clearly headed toward collapse in any case."[68]

The breakdown of the Soviet empire was sanctioned by an edict from the Russian Parliament—an edict that suspended any and all activities of the Communist Party on August 30, 1991. Almost immediately after this step, the individual republics followed suit, closing the offices of the Communist Party and confiscating all its properties and funds.

In contrast to empires that dissolved in a historical process, lasting for decades or even centuries (for example, the Ottoman Empire), the decaying and exhausted Soviet political order fell apart within days, with the institutions at the center transformed into insignificant structures on Yeltsin's orders. At the same time, Gorbachev—on the way out as president of a nonexistent country[69]—was stripped of the special powers mandated by decree in 1990.

With the rapid demise of the totalitarian-bureaucratic machine and the moribund Communist ideology—now a bankrupt political force—"the failed coup legitimized the claim of post-Communist reformers that they are the rightful heirs to power, and invigorated them for the mammoth task of civilizing their country."[70] However, one of the major roadblocks in the way of civilizing this splintered post-Soviet community of nations is the absence of democratic traditions, customs, and habits, so instrumental in recognizing the virtues of the unenforceable—the unwritten social rules, such as mutual trust and respect for fellow human beings. Of course, not only recognition but also obedience to the unenforceable rules depends largely on the willingness of the citizenry to accept these rules as truth—a truth that guarantees the survival of a decent society.

However, the creation of a decent society is only a precondition in the quest for a workable democratic system. This kind of political enterprise is characterized by men living together in a society in which political liberties—manifested, above all, in the active presence of opposing parties—represent the crucial test of a democratic system. Another important presupposition of a democratic society is expressed in the frequently used phrase "the essential dignity and worth of man," which is understood to mean that human dignity and worth are demonstrated in people's ability to make free choices in a deliberate, rational manner. But to make "deliberate, rational choices" in a democratic society requires a set of attitudes, such as a desire to be self-governing, a confidence in the political system and its policies, a willingness to participate in the political process, a considerable willingness to compromise, and, finally, a high value placed on peace and order, achieved through institutionalized political freedoms.[71]

To be sure, the reality of a democratically structured society brings with it the possibility of misguided emotional appeals, manipulation, and resentment. There is even the risk of demagoguery—a demagoguery that panders to the passions and unconcealed prejudices of the people. And it is these dangers and risks that threaten the renewal of post-Communist societies, which are still reeling under the impact of the Soviet imperial legacy. The political effects of this imperial legacy are twofold: On the one hand, the people of czarist Russia, with the exception of the few months of the short-lived February Revolution, never experienced life under freely elected democratic governments. During long centuries, these peoples were landlocked both in spirit and in the social forms of the autocratic state. Deprived of all freedom to act in the public arena, they rarely attempted to break out of the oppressive reign of the czarist patriarchy. On the other hand, three generations of Soviet citizens have grown up and lived under the totalitarian regime of a ruthless and unscrupulous Communist Party. In either case, the absence of democratic traditions makes the transfer to a more liberal system of government a formidable task. And this is the major reason that the lasting impact of the Soviet imperial legacy can once more change the business of politics into a sinister play.

Furthermore, it is sometimes overlooked that the dissolution of the Communist Party does not necessarily mean the final demise of its organization and functions. In Soviet political life, there had been, since Lenin, always a duplicate state power apparatus, a "double structure—established in every sphere of life and on all levels: national, district, regional [and] local . . . overseeing and directing every aspect of work in accordance with ideological requirements from top to bottom, in order to guarantee that each party directive will be carried out to the letter."[72]

It is noteworthy that when, according to news dispatches, the republics seized the assets and funds of the outlawed Communist Parties, in some cases this "shadow government" did immediately replace the apparatchiks and served as a substitute for the party, abandoning the ideological trappings but retaining a strong grip on political and economic power. For example, in Uzbekistan, a journalist reported that "there is no sign of the democratic overthrow of communism" and that the republic remains under the control of former Communists who have conveniently discarded the ideological icons. In fact, the Uzbek president declared that "Uzbekistan would follow the Chinese model of economic reform, because it (the republic) was not ready for full democracy or a market economy."[73]

Similar developments were reported from Tajikistan, Azerbaijan, and Turkmenistan, with former Communists consolidating power by appealing to raw nationalism. The president of Ukraine, Leonid Kravchuk—a former Communist—recognized the Emergency Committee during the first two days of the coup, then, suddenly declaring his opposition to its ringleaders, jumped on the nationalist bandwagon, proclaiming his pro-independence sympathies.[74] Even in the newly emancipated Russian Federation, where Yeltsin is trying hard to extinguish the remnants of the Communist infrastructure, people are expressing their contempt for "the so-called democrats who after being elected to office proved more adept at feathering their nests than attending to the grievances of their constituents."[75]

According to Giovanni Sartori, the grand event of our times—"the implosion of communism"—is "in its wake a two-step process: 1) the exit from a dictatorship, and 2) the entry into a democratic form. The exit has been, to everybody's surprise, the easy part; the entry turns out to be, not unpredictably, the difficult one."[76]

And if we consider the entry into the democratic fold, we have to pose the following question: Is it possible to liberalize a former empire that dissolved itself into a group of national republics, which—apart from many other formidable problems—have to struggle with the perplexities of nation building and state building? The answer to this question depends largely on a commitment to democracy—a commitment to a pluralist political structure dedicated not only to the pragmatic interaction of political parties, but also to the individual with his unalienable rights within the universal human family. And in assessing the role of the individual in the newly emancipated republics, we have to take into consideration one of the major afflictions visited on the peoples of the former USSR: the "logic of fatigue" experienced after more than seven decades of indoctrination and ideological warfare—a process that invented its own drab language of derogatory words and smear tactics against the West, along with the relentless barrage of Marxist-Leninist slogans parroted by people as substitutes for reasoning. It is because of this "logic of fatigue" that the leaders of the fledgling democracies "are having a hard time persuading people to take advantage of their new rights and observe their basic civic duties."[77]

However, the democratization process—very uneven and nebulous in some areas—is only a part of the intense efforts of some republican leaders to prevent things from getting out of control. Thus there is the problem of regional fragmentation, with a number of subset "autonomous" republics, such as Tatarstan and Mordova, demanding real autonomy, assuring ethnic hegemony, and incorporating the exclusive ownership of raw materials and economic property. Furthermore, there is the problem of how the nonimperial, post-Soviet community can create viable and lasting relationships among the republics, in view of the unresolved questions of borders, territorial jurisdiction, and armies and navies. And what about the problem related to the status of ethnic Russians—25 to 40% of whom live outside the territory of Russia proper? And finally, what will be the fate of the nuclear arsenals scattered all over the territory of the former Soviet empire?

But above all, the post-Soviet community of nations—still quite far from a victory for democracy—faces intractable economic problems calling for radical reforms and painful solutions. The overall economy is in a state of chaos, plagued by shortages, while money is less and less acceptable as a means of exchange. Declining efficiency in production is caused by the lackadaisical work ethic, best explained by the joke inherited from the Communist regime: "They pretend to pay us; we pretend to work." In some areas there is a scarcity of vital consumer goods due to the lack of raw materials, a state of affairs attributed to the absence of coordination extended to commercial contracts and the failure to settle contentious issues among the republics. As the economist Anders Aslund notes, "republics, enterprises, and individuals simply refuse to deliver to each other."[78] Needless to say, this condition is encouraging extensive barter economics—a development hardly conducive to a free market system.

Wages have dropped so low in contrast to the enormous price increases that a majority of people now live well below the subsistence level, while the army of the unemployed is steadily growing. The old-style mentality persists in considering the state as an enemy, as an institution to be cheated. In consequence, new private companies pay only a fraction of the outstanding taxes, adding billions of rubles to budgetary deficits "in addition" to the "budget burden of writing off debts of collective and state farms" operating at a loss.[79] Moreover, the absence of a clear-cut, effective monetary policy and the collapse of state revenues are due largely to the lack of crucial levers of control on the republican as well as on the provincial level.

To make matters worse, "corruption has reached unheard-of proportions" and, according to reports from Moscow, "bribery finds in capitalism the beginnings of a beautiful friendship."[80] It seems that thanks to their connections, many factory managers—most of them former Communists—are "opening doors and their pockets to privatization deals that will assure them a future in the market economy."[81]

However, even aboveboard dealings with the privatization process in the former Soviet Union meet with opposition to "market ethics, particularly about the market's indifference to 'equality' and 'justice,' and the market actors' use of material self-interest (interpreted as greed) as their principal incentive."[82]

With the virtual institutionalization of envy, there is also the impression that if someone is successful in business, he must have achieved that success by immoral or illegal means. Moreover, there is also the fear of privatization, with workers and consumers asking for protection in their aversion to "the market system [which] rewards individual success in fulfilling the needs of others."[83] Disregarding the fact that a planned command (nonmarket) economy is clearly inferior to a private, free, market-established economy, the fear of privatization was engendered in more than seventy years of Communist rule which created the *Homo Sovieticus*, "a sheltered man, a human being hostile to, and scared by, the risks and uncertainties of the open society and its competitive race."[84]

Of course, the post-Communist societies—so attracted to the abundance of goods in the West—will have to outgrow the "logic of fatigue" and the "fear of privatization" in a process of transition and renewal. The core issue is how soon Marxist-Leninist ideas and views will be replaced in this process—a process of transformation that will encourage risk taking, initiative, and innovation—creating a climate favorable to free enterprise and commerce in a working democracy.

Seemingly, the stresses and strains are so widespread in the Commonwealth of Independent States that the predominant attitude is one of anxious and pessimistic uncertainty about what the future has in store. In exasperation, the Russian political scientist Vyacheslav Kostikov concluded that "in matters of democracy we are closer to the Neanderthal man than to *Homo Sapiens*."[85] In contrast, a great number of Yeltsin supporters, disunited as they are, exhibit more confidence in their ability to cope with the complex problems of democratization and social reconstruction. Apparently, in this crisis and tension of human affairs, all that is needed is the moral support for the foundations for a decent society and trust in the advantages of developing democratic institutions. Of course, this democratization process also calls, in the long run, for leadership, patience, perseverance, and general consciousness raising, so that the *Homo sapiens* might prevail.

Notes

1. Cited in Anatole Shub, "The Fourth Russian Revolution—Historical Perspectives," *Problems of Communism* (Nov.–Dec., 1991): 20.
2. John Dewey, *Reconstruction in Philosophy* (Boston: Beacon Press, 1962), vi.
3. Cited in Richard Pipes, "Russia's Chance," *Commentary* (March 1992): 29.
4. Peter Reddaway, "The End of the Empire," *New York Review of Books* (Nov. 7, 1991), 55.
5. As the renowned sociologist Pitrim Sorokin observed, "there is no government with such an enormous quantity of corruption, of thieves, unprincipled scoundrels who spill blood in order to obtain wealth and who disguise their crimes by proclaiming high ideals." *The Sociology of Revolution* (New York: Howard Fertig, 1967), 160, n. 42.
6. Giovanni Sartori, "Rethinking Democracy: Bad Polity and Bad Politics," *International Social Science Journal* (August, 1991): 439.
7. Lenin's scientific definition of dictatorship, cited in Mikhail Heller and Alexander Nekrich, *Utopia in Power* (New York: Summit Books, 1986), 62. Henceforth referred to as *Utopia in Power*.
8. Charles H. Fairbanks, Jr., "The Nature of the Beast," *National Interest* (Spring 1993): 51.
9. Creating what George Kennan called a "culture of pretense." Cited in Ralph Dahrendorf, *Reflections on the Revolution in Europe* (New York: Times Books, 1990), 24.
10. *Utopia in Power*, 533.
11. Ibid., 529.
12. Ernst A. Menze, ed., *Totalitarianism Reconsidered* (Port Washington, N.Y.: Kennikot Press, 1981), 22.
13. Frederick Barghorn and Thomas Remington, *Politics in the USSR* (Boston: Little, Brown, and Co., 1986), 277.
14. The journal *Problems of Communism* (May-June, 1977) has devoted nine pages to the review of six Soviet books (1972-1974) on the scientific management of society.
15. Boris Toporkin, *The New Constitution of the USSR* (Moscow: Progress Publishers, 1977), 238.

16. *The Programme of the Communist Party of the Soviet Union* (Moscow: Novosti Press Agency, 1986), 6.
17. Leonard Shapiro, ed., *The USSR and the Future* (New York: Frederick A. Praeger, 1963), 262.
18. *The Programme of the Communist Party* (1986), 24. Emphasis added.
19. Iurii Afanas'ev, "Perestroika and Historical Knowledge," *Michigan Quarterly Review* (Fall 1989): 541.
20. Ibid., 544.
21. Martin Malia, "A New Russian Revolution?" *New York Review of Books* (July 18, 1991): 29.
22. The text of the lengthy resolution was published in *Pravda* on July 5, 1988.
23. Ibid.
24. The literal translation of *glasnost* is "publicity." However, the translation is problematical and there are sound arguments for a number of alternatives. One alternative, "openness," comes closest to conveying the cornerstone of Gorbachev's new policy.
25. Moshe Levin, *The Gorbachev Phenomenon* (Berkeley: University of California Press, 1988), x.
26. Toporkin, *New Constitution*, 271. In reality, the Supreme Soviet amounted to a rubber-stamp "parliamentary" body.
27. Severyn Bialer, ed., *Politics, Society, and Nationality Inside Gorbachev's Russia* (Boulder, Colo.: Westview Press, 1989), 122.
28. Gorbachev's speech at the U.N., *Pravda*, Dec. 8, 1988, 1.
29. Peter Juviler, "Human Rights and Perestroika: Progress and Perils," *The Harriman Institute Forum*, 4, no. 6 (June, 1991): 1.
30. Ibid.
31. John Gooding, "Gorbachev and Democracy," *Soviet Studies* 42, no. 2 (April, 1990): 196. The last quotation Gooding attributed to Robert C. Tucker.
32. Mikhail Gorbachev, *Selected Speeches and Articles* (Moscow: Progress Publishers, 1987), 59.
33. Cited in *Midstream* (February–March, 1991): 18.
34. Cited in Joseph Schull, "The Self-Destruction of Soviet Ideology," *The Harriman Institute Forum* 4, no. 7 (July 1991): 6. Emphasis added.
35. Ibid., 3.
36. Cited in Raymond Taras, "The Makings of a Leninist: Gorbachev on Dogmatism and Revisionism," *Studies in Soviet Thought* 42 (1991): 19.
37. Ibid.
38. Cited in Charles H. Fairbanks, Jr., "The Suicide of Soviet Communism," *Journal of Democracy* 1, no. 2 (Spring 1990): 18–19.
39. Ibid., 20.
40. Ibid., 25 and passim.
41. *The Current Digest of the Soviet Press* XLII, no. 49 (1990): 2; excerpt from *Pravda* (Dec. 9, 1990). Henceforth referred to as *Current Digest*.
42. *Current Digest* XLII, no. 36 (1990): 15.

43. Marina Pavlova-Silvanskaya, "Real Processes Don't Want to Follow Armchair Prescriptions," *Izvestia* (Sept. 24, 1990): 3.
44. Ibid.
45. Cited in Juviler, "Human Rights and Perestroika," 1.
46. *Current Digest* XLIII, no. 17 (1991): 7.
47. Gorbachev again ignored the excision of Article 6 from the Constitution.
48. *Current Digest* XLIII, no. 17 (1991): 7. Excerpt from *Pravda*, April 26, 1991.
49. Ibid., 11.
50. Amy Knight, "The Coup That Never Was: Gorbachev and the Forces of Reaction," *Problems of Communism* (Nov.–Dec., 1991): 39.
51. Ibid., 36.
52. Ibid., 39.
53. William E. Odom, "Alternative Perspectives on the August Coup," *Problems of Communism* (Nov.–Dec., 1991): 15.
54. Shub, "The Fourth Russian Revolution," 21.
55. Odom, "Alternative Perspectives," 15.
56. Malcolm Mackintosh, "The New Russian Revolution—The military dimension," *Conflict Studies* (January, 1992): 8. Henceforth referred to as *Conflict*.
57. Knight, "The Coup That Never Was," 39.
58. Mark R. Beisinger, "The Deconstruction of the USSR and the Search for a Post-Soviet Community," *Problems of Communism* (Nov.–Dec., 1991): 28.
59. Ibid.
60. Odom, "Alternative Perspectives," 14.
61. Cited in Abraham Brumberg, "The Road to Minsk," *New York Review of Books* (January 30, 1992): 21.
62. "When the coup developed, a good number of senior officers in both the military and the KGB sided with Yeltsin" (cited in Anders Aslund, "Russia's Road from Communism," *Daedalus* [Spring 1992]: 82).
63. *Conflict*, 9.
64. Knight, "The Coup That Never Was," 40.
65. Odom, "Alternative Perspectives," 13.
66. Michael Bukowski, "Collapsible Communism," *Soviet Analyst* 21, no. 3 (January, 1992): 6.
67. Reddaway, "The End of the Empire," 54.
68. Beisinger, "Deconstruction of the USSR," 27.
69. *Current Digest* XLIII, no. 51 (1991): 6. Interestingly, the mainline Sovietologist Jerry Hough, in his long article "Gorbachev's Endgame" (*World Policy Journal* [Fall 1990]), insisted that "Gorbachev has been in firm control of the reform process and, assuming he stays healthy, he is almost certain to remain in power at least until the 1995 presidential election" (cited by Reddaway, "The End of the Empire," 59).
70. Bill Keller, "Old Guard's Last Gasp," *New York Times* (August 22, 1991): 1.

71. H. B. Mayo, *An Introduction to Democratic Theory* (New York and Oxford: Oxford University Press, 1977).
72. Vladimir Bukovsky, "Will Gorbachev Reform the Soviet Union?" *Commentary* (Sept., 1986): 20.
73. Reddaway, "The End of the Empire," 53.
74. Brumberg, "The Road to Minsk," 22.
75. Ibid., 21.
76. Sartori, "Rethinking Democracy," 438.
77. Stephan Engelberg, "East Bloc Treading Water in a Sinkhole of Lethargy," *The New York Times* (April 8, 1992): A-14.
78. Anders Aslund, "The Soviet Economy After the Coup," *Problems of Communism* (Nov-Dec., 1991): 44.
79. Ibid., 45.
80. Celestine Bohlen, "Corruption Grows Greedy in Russia," *New York Times* (March 14, 1992): 4.
81. Ibid.
82. Jan S. Prybyla, "The Road From Socialism: Why, Where, What and How," *Problems of Communism* (Jan.–April, 1991): 4.
83. Ibid., 5.
84. Sartori, "Rethinking Democracy," 446.
85. Vyacheslav Kostikov, "Novaya Nomenklatura: Blesk Nishchety" (New Bureaucracy: The Glitter of Poverty), *Ogoniok* 8 (February, 1992): 7. At present, Mr. Kostikov is a spokesman for President Yeltsin.

Postscript
Early February, 1994

In the aftermath of the December 12, 1993, elections, Russia is at a dramatic crossroads, facing a gridlock of problems that can be resolved only in an atmosphere of political stability and economic progress. However, with the Communist old guard (posing as democrats) reasserting political dominance, the tasks of financial and economic reconstruction have suffered a serious setback. It is not surprising that these newly baked "democrats" are now labeling the efforts of yesterday's reformers as a case of "market romanticism."[1] Incapable of extricating Russia from its imperial past and representing powerful reactionary interests, these Communist stalwarts are best characterized by Vladimir Bukovsky in this way:

> Most of them regard the recent events in Russia not as a revolution liberating the people from totalitarian oppression and requiring a vision of a conceptually different future, but rather as a natural continuation of their careers within the same old hierarchy. Clinging to power with Lenin-like tenacity, they will never allow anything new and healthy to prosper in Russia because they do not see a need for anything new and healthy. Democracy means for them nothing more than a field for deception and manipulation, just as the market economy amounts in their eyes only to one thing: corruption. Consequently, they will always treat any genuine private initiative as corruption, while justifying their own corruption by the workings of the market economy.[2]

Even more dangerous—because it touches deep-seated popular sentiments—is the old guard's vigorous commitment to neo-imperialism, a form of aggressiveness mixed with great power nostalgia.

Obviously, the projected radical slowdown of reforms by the old guard, which is now heading the key ministries, will find strong support in the newly elected lower Parliament, where deputies from the reformist factions total 164 while those from the hardline ultra-nationalist and Communist parties total 182. However, to prevent any considerable slowdown of badly needed reforms, the newly adapted Constitution—an amalgam of U.S. and French systems—gives Yeltsin legislative initiatives that favor executive power with appropriate decrees and vetoes of regressive legislation. Still, to work within the framework of constitutional politics consistent with political stability in a reformed market economy, Yeltsin will have to prove that he is a champion of change without bloodshed and that he is a defender of democratic liberties—liberties that are guaranteed by democratic institutions and a nationwide consensus. But above all, in order to counter accusations of authoritarianism and reverse Bolshevism,[3] Yeltsin will have to understand that in a society guided by democratic principles, "power must always feel the check of power."[4]

Notes

1. *New York Times* (January 30, 1994): E–5.
2. Vladimir Bukovsky's letter to *Commentary* (October, 1993): 11.
3. Robert V. Daniels, "The Riddle of Russian Reform," *Dissent* (Fall 1993): 489–96.
4. Justice Louis Brandeis, cited in *Midstream* (December, 1993): 16.

Index

Afanas'ev, V. G., 101–3
Akhromeyev, Sergey, (Marshal), 148
Alexandrov, G. F., 115
Amalrik, A., 68
Andropov, Yuri, 25, 141, 143
apparatchiks, 12–13, 23, 147
Aristotle, 26
Aslund, Anders, 154
authoritarianism, 8, 68
authoritarian model, 14

Bacon, Francis, xii, 38–39, 42; *Novum Organum*, 38
barrack socialism, 17
Berlin, Isaiah, 75–76
Bialer, Severyn, 14
Bolsheviks, 82–84, 86, 97, 112, 139–40
Breslauer, George W., 15–16
Brezhnev, Leonid, 11, 25, 100–101, 141
Brezhnev Constitution 1977, 85–86
Brezhnev Doctrine, 131–32, 135
Brzezinski, Zbigniew, 13, 15–16, 20–21, 141
Bukovsky, Vladimir, 161

censorship, 19, 143
Central Committee of the Communist Party of the Soviet Union, 112–13, 115, 141, 145, 147
CHEKA (All Russian Commission for Suppression of Counterrevolution, Sabotage and Speculation), 84
civil society, 12, 73
class struggle, 45–47, 50, 54, 58, 78, 81, 98, 121, 135
Cohen, Stephen F., 8n22, 66n6
coherence theory, 40
collectivism, 22, 99–102
collectivization, 25, 140
communism, 66, 78, 97–98, 102–4, 110–11, 130, 142–43
communist elite, 12, 14, 66–67, 99, 104
communist morality, 95, 99
Communist Party of the Soviet Union (CPSU), 5, 13, 15, 19, 21–24, 57, 73, 84–85, 93–97, 109–10, 113–14, 121–23, 131, 140–41, 143, 147, 151–52; Twentieth Congress, 116; Twenty-second Congress, 96; Twenty-fifth Congress, 100–101, 122; Twenty-seventh Congress, 142
concentration camps, 85, 140
Congress of People's Deputies, 143, 145
Conquest, Robert, 15
copy theory, 55, 117
correspondence theory, 40
Council for Mutual Economic Assistance (CMEA), 132–35

163

Deborin, A. M., 111–12
democracy, 69–70, 73–74, 76–78, 83, 85, 130, 153
democratic centralism, 85
development theory, 9
Dewey, John, 43–47, 139; *Logic: The Theory of Inquiry*, 43
dialectic, 54, 71, 111, 122–23, 129
dialectical materialism, 44–45, 93, 110–11, 116–17, 120–23
dialectical method, 119
dictatorship of the proletariat, 68, 80
dissidents, 23, 25

elections, 12–13, 66
Engels, Friedrich, 33, 46, 48, 50, 53, 55, 68, 76–77, 79, 95, 112–13
ethics, 56, 94–95

Fairbanks, Charles H., Jr., 145
fascism, 21
Feuerbach, Ludwig, 33, 36–37
Friedgut, Theodore H., 12–13
Friedrich, Carl J., 20–21
Fromm, Erich, 71–72

George, Richard T. de, 94
glasnost, 109, 142–43
Goldman, Marshall J., 15
Gorbachev, Mikhail, 11–12, 141, 143–44, 146–51
Gramsci, Antonio, 57
Graziani, Giovanni, 134
Gromyko, Andrei, 131
groupthink, 56
GULAG (acronym for the Main Administration of Correction Labor Camps), 149

Hegel, Georg W. F., 41, 56, 75, 112
Heine, Heinrich, 81
historical materialism, 35, 93, 117–23
Hobbes, Thomas, xiii

Hoffman, Erik P., 8, 14
Homo Sovieticus, 17, 155
Hook, Sidney, 44–45, 70, 73
horizontal concepts, 19
Hough, Jerry, 16
Hughes, H. Stuart, 79

ideology, xiii–xiv, 18–21, 24–25, 45, 73, 86, 94, 98, 103, 110, 114, 120, 123, 129–30, 140
industrialization, 4
Institute of Red Professors, 110
instrumentalism, 43–45

Juviler, Peter, 144

Kerensky, Alexander, 139
KGB (Committee for State Security), 146–50
Khrushchev, Nikita, 5, 132, 140–41; *Khrushchev Remembers* (memoir), 141; Secret Speech at the Twentieth Congress, 140
Klyamkin, Igor, 4
knowledge, 7, 9–10, 14, 33–34, 36, 38–40, 42–47, 52, 55, 99
Kolakowski, Leszek, 17, 24, 72
Konwicki, Tadeusz, 67
Kostikov, Vyacheslav, 155
Kravchuk, Leonid, 153
Kryuchkov, Vladimir, 148
Kuhn, Thomas S., 9, 15
kulak, 112

Lamont, Corliss, 44–45
Lane, David, 66
Lenin, V. I., 4, 37, 55, 57, 68–69, 72, 78, 81–85, 93, 98, 110–11, 113, 120, 130, 144; *Materialism and Empirio-criticism*, 55; *State and Revolution*, 83; *The Tasks of Russian Social Democrats*, 82–83
Leonhard, Wolfgang, 5
logic of fatigue, 153–55
Lovell, David W., 68
Lukacs, George, 55, 112

Machiavelli, Niccolo, xii
McWilliams, Wilson Carey, xv
Malia, Martin (Z), 3, 142; "To the Stalin Mausoleum," 3, 6–7, 18
Manning, D. J., 69
Marx, Karl, xi, 33–39, 41–52, 54–57, 68–82, 95, 112, 113, 120; *Address of the Central Committee to the Communist League*, 47–50, 78; *Communist Manifesto*, 46–48, 78; *Critique of the Gotha Program*, 79; *Critique of Hegel's Philosophy of Right*, 70, 75–77; *Economic and Philosophical Manuscripts of 1844*, 51, 55, 75, 81; *The German Ideology*, 33–34; *Theses on Feuerbach*, 33–34, 43–48, 51–52
Marxism, xi, xiii, 44–48, 52, 54–56, 69–70, 73, 97, 111, 113
Marxism-Leninism, 4–5, 17–18, 22, 24, 26, 57–58, 66, 86, 93–94, 97, 101, 103, 110, 112, 116, 119, 120, 122–24, 140, 142
matter, 116–17, 122
Matthews, Mervyn, 105
Maynard, John, 69
mechanists, 111–12
Menshevizing idealism, 111–12
methodological revolution, 10, 12
Michnik, Adam, 12
Milosz, Czeslav, 20, 109
Ministry of Internal Affairs (MVD), 147, 149–50
Mitin, M. B., 113–14
mode of production, 38, 119, 130
modernization, 13, 15
Moral Code of the Builder of Communism, 96–98, 100–101, 103, 105

neo-Stalinism, 5, 12, 17, 20
new Soviet man, 8, 22, 94, 97, 103
nomenklatura, 19

Odom, E. William, 149
O'Malley, Joseph, 70

Orwell, George, 16, 20; *1984*, 20

parliamentarism, 83
party principle (*partyinost*), 110, 112, 115, 121–22
Pasternak, Boris, 62–63n82
Peirce, C. S., 44
perestroika, xiv, 3, 12, 109, 143–44, 146, 148
perspectivism, 70
philosophy, 39–40, 43, 45–46, 52, 57, 109–16, 120–21
Pipes, Richard, 15
Plamenatz, John, 125
Plato, xii
Plekhanov, Georgi, 54, 111
pluralism, 9, 11–12
polis, xii
power, 67, 73, 81, 99, 162
pragmatism, 43
Pravda (newspaper), 101, 131, 145
praxis (practice), xiii, 34–39, 41, 51–58, 112
production relations, 118, 135
productive forces of society, 118, 135
proletarian power, 121
purges, 16–17, 114, 132, 140

Remnick, David, 4
re-Stalinization, 141
Revolution: February 1917, 139, 152; October 1917, 54, 83, 85, 110, 120
revolutionary practice, 33, 47, 48–49, 52, 54–55, 123
Robespierre, Maximilien, 81
Robinson, T. J., 69
Rothman, Stanley, 15
Rousseau, Jean Jacques, 81
Rubel, Maximilien, 71
Russell, Bertrand, 44
Rutland, Peter, 9

Sakharov, Andrei, 148
Samizdat, 25
Sanakoyev, Salva, 132–33